Westward the Bells

A biography of Junipero Serra

by Marion F. Sullivan

St. Paul Books & Media

Library of Congress Cataloging-in-Publication Data
Sullivan, Marion F.
   Westward the bells / written by Marion F. Sullivan. —Abridged ed.
      p.   cm.
   Bibliography: p.
   ISBN 0-8198-8227-5 (pbk.)
    1. Serra, Junípero 1713-1784. 2. Indians of North America—California—
Missions.   3. Explorers—California—Biography.   4. Explorers—Spain—
Biography. 5. Franciscans—California—Biography. 6. California—History
—To 1846. I. Title.
F864.S44S852 1988
979.4'02'0924—dc19
[B]   88-23853
                                              CIP

Printed in the U.S.A., by the Daughters of St. Paul
50 St. Paul's Ave., Boston, MA 02130

The Daughters of St. Paul are an international congregation of women
religious serving the Church with the communications media.

1 2 3 4 5 6 7 8 9   96 95 94 93 92 91 90 89 88

Dedicated
to my husband
C. Edward Sullivan

Contents

Content

Preface

The story of Father Junipero Serra has been many times told. But perhaps today, as never before, his impressive works and magnanimous soul radiate drama on the stage of history and stir our hearts. For as we look into the past, we see in the life of this illustrious leader a poignant relationship to our own problems— the problems of today, tomorrow and always.

I wish to express particular gratitude to the Academy of American Franciscan History and especially to Father Maynard Geiger, O.F.M., Ph.D., and Father Antonine Tibesar, O.F.M., Ph.D., whose tireless research and fine works have not only revealed facts heretofore unknown but also clarified familiar ones. To the many others close to me, who have given their help, advice and encouragement, I am most grateful. I wish to give special mention to my friend and faithful helper, Mrs. Evelyn Ullrich.

I have attempted to emphasize Serra's heritage and the motivating forces that destined him to push Christian civilization to the far Pacific shores of the North American continent. The ancient bells of Palma echo their song of love today in San Diego, Santa Barbara and Carmel.

Letters
of Gold

A bell rang out at dawn, calling the Angelus. Then from the distant hills, from the great cathedral, from more than half-a-hundred churches, convents and chapels in and around the Mediterranean city of Palma they resounded—round, solemn, resonant bells; sharp, blithe, soprano bells mingling with tiny tinkling chimes. Their message vibrated, bounded and rolled over red-tiled, flat-roofed houses, colorful gardens, Islamic domes and Gothic towers, and drifted down to the curving shores of the sparkling aqua bay, to fade beyond—somewhere in the western sea.

Chroniclers of the day, these bells would ring intermittently for morning Masses, a wedding, a funeral or the proclamation of important news. Life in Palma synchronized with bells. Today they seemed to ring with intensity, as though anticipating drama for this capital city of Majorca.

Fr. Junípero Serra had long since risen from his narrow plank bed. As long as he could remember, his days had been regulated by the reassuring immutability of bells. The dim light of early morning crept in to reveal the barrenness of his monastery cell in the Convent of St. Francis, as he knelt in prayer. Like an undulant sea, his mind was surging with tumultuous cross currents. But the vital problems dominating his consciousness were personal. Consequently, he left them to the ultimate plan of God and turned his immediate attention to the neatly formulated program of the day.

It was January 25, the feast day of Blessed Ramón Lull. In 1749, as she had for four hundred years, Spain would turn back the pages of her romantic history to honor a loved national hero and Christian martyr. But Majorcans in particular regarded this as one of the greatest celebrations of the year. Lull was their own native son. Born in Palma in 1235, he lay buried in the church of St. Francis. The annual festivities provided a tangible testament of personal affection for this man.

Today the usually tranquil Palma bustled with activity. Most everyone was hanging banners, arranging flower festoons, polishing or furbishing the already neat, gem-like little city. It must sparkle! Guests of importance would be coming. The celebration would be no boisterous, noisy fiesta. Music and dancing would come later, but the morning activities, in keeping with their intention, would be religious, patriotic and academic.

Though most Palmans had no direct contact with the university, it represented their aspirations. They loved the venerable institution and its traditions. It had given Palma much of its character and its charm. Named for the famous Majorcan Franciscan, the fifteenth-century Lullian University of Palma had been officially recognized in 1673 by Pope Clement X, with the impressive title "Pontifical Imperial Royal and Literary University of Majorca." For the sake of simplicity, however, it was generally known as the University of Palma.

Today the university would flash her elegance and splendor in traditionally dramatic pageantry. Reliving valiant and heroic deeds performed for God and country, she would coordinate the cherished past with the vital present, making them one in the living spirit of the holy Catholic faith, the life, the soul of the Spanish world.

People had been asking, "Who is to be the speaker of the day?" Always, it was one of the important speeches of the year. This year, chosen for the honor was the illustrious head of the department of theology at the Lullian University of Palma, Friar Minor of the Order of St. Francis, the Reverend Junípero Serra.

News traveled fast, even in 1749. Nobles, statesmen, intellectuals, guildsmen, farmers, laborers, everyone applauded the choice. They knew this brilliant educator, this leading and widely acclaimed theologian, this warmly loved, humble son of St. Francis. A native of Petra, twenty-five miles away, Serra had come to Palma in his early teens. Now, at thirty-five, he had spent more than half his life in the lovely center of Christian devotion, culture and knowledge. Under the gentle guidance of learned Franciscans, he had graduated from novice to priest, from student to distinguished professor, eminent scholar and eloquent speaker.

Majorcans knew Serra and he knew them. They loved the jovial Franciscan. His easy manner, his kindness and his quick natural sense of humor made him a friend to everyone. Only about five feet, two inches tall and pleasantly plump, he had a kindly, rotund face which framed brown, twinkling eyes that could reach into the depths of another's with thoughtful concern and loving understanding.

Fr. Serra never sought personal honors, glory or fame. He seemed unaware of the aura of acclaim attributed to him. Furthermore, even those who ardently sang his praises could not comprehend his profound capacity for love. For from love alone emanated his words of wisdom.

For generations Serra's people had lived by the soil, and his academic life had never diminished his awareness of this valuable heritage. The hopes of budding spring, the cruel deprivation of drought, the rewarding satisfaction of an abundant harvest, the tragedy of plague, all were bred in the roots and blood of agrarian Majorcans. This heritage of intimate contact with nature, one of his greatest riches, not only united Serra with the people of his homeland, but would in the years to come become an invaluable source of physical and moral strength.

Outshining all other qualities was his glowing religious zeal, which engendered warmth and understanding, compassion and tenderness reaching from the pulpit to the cries and heartaches of his people. In the classroom and throughout the entire island, when lenten missions or special feast day sermons had taken him to the other cities and villages of Majorca, his words reached into the souls of men, bringing them peace and communion with God. When he was to speak, crowds filled the churches. People strained to hear every word, then told their friends about the Franciscan with the resonant, musical voice, yet so strangely gentle, who could "talk on anything from rocks to eternity."[1]

No doubt, this appointment as speaker for the festivities of Ramón Lull gave Fr. Serra some natural pleasure, some exaltation of recognition. We can only be certain, however, that he would have accepted the assignment with characteristic humility. The sermon was his responsibility of the day, but Serra's mind was in conflict with other problems. It had been so for months.

These problems concerned his deepest being, all he had been, all he hoped to be. They challenged his vocation to the priesthood and its essence, the salvation of souls. Vocation is part calling and part listening. He was praying and listening. He was praying and listening and watching for answers.

Even before his novitiate, Serra had read everything he could about St. Francis and his early companions. These men had become his close friends. The vicarious friendship had not only developed a deep reverence for the founders of the Franciscan Order but had also directed an intense personal desire to bring the faith to the thousands who had not yet heard the Word of God. He wanted to become a missionary, and should God find him worthy, to become a martyr for Christ.

Martyrdom, perhaps, was a daring aspiration. But missionary work had been the propelling motive of his vocation. It had triggered his application to every aspect of his intellectual and spiritual development. Paths had opened before him, and he had followed sedulously, knowing interiorly that all comes from God. The positions he now held, the honors, the esteem were not of his seeking, but natural products of his thirty-five

---

1. Geiger, *The Life and Times of Junípero Serra*, Vol. VI, p. 33.

years of activity: fruits following bloom. We can look back and assume they were inevitable.

Serra was no idealistic dreamer. Before he spoke to anyone of his desire, he must be certain it was no personal whim, no urge born of sudden, over-zealous fascination. He met the problem in the only way he knew. He prayed. The flames grew. He prayed, too, for a companion, someone like himself, who desired missionary work. And each day the calling grew in intensity.

He could foresee his colleagues' reactions, should the news circulate. They would say he was indispensable to the university; no one could replace him; after all these years of Franciscan training, he was obligated to the university; he would be casting away rewards due his life's labors. Greater honors for him were already rumored. And they would also say he was too old. Thirty-five was late to start a new and hazardous career.

There was another stumbling block. Majorcan priests had been prohibited from missionary work in the New World. It was a political situation. Traditionally independent Majorca had resisted the Spanish Crown, submitting only around 1709. And long ago a Majorcan missionary had failed. For forty years not one missionary preparatory school had been established in Majorca and no Majorcans had served in the New World.

But Serra knew the fine army of dedicated and qualified Franciscans who, given the opportunity, would serve valiantly in the field. He knew also that the existence of a situation for forty years did not make it impervious to change.

He had surveyed the field realistically and made his plans.

First he had told his superior, who would need time to find a replacement. No records indicate the superior's reactions to the interview. His later actions, however, suggest that Serra's apprehensions were justified. Serra told no one else. His thoughts were too deeply serious for idle discussion, alarm or fanfare. He had pledged his superior to secrecy and awaited developments.

Alone in his cell, Serra weighed these problems, then turned to the task of the day, his talk on Ramón Lull. The saintly fellow-Majorcan was one of his favorite heroes. He could hardly have studied history, philosophy and theology without an intimate knowledge of Ramón Lull. To tell others of him would be a natural revelation of inspiring deeds, ideas, and ideals.

Bells shattered the monastic silence. Reverberating through corridors and cloisters, they proclaimed the time—ten o'clock—the hour for the ceremonies to begin.

Members of the faculty, priests and students were milling about the courtyard. A bugle blast, a sharp command from the beadle, and military order prevailed. Double symmetrical lines of academic caps and gowns formed a sea of dignified black, splashed with silk-lined hoods and drapes of red, blue, purple, gold and white, designating special honors, degrees and departments. Gray-robed Franciscans, priests in black cassocks with white albs and first year students in black tailored suits followed, all slowly moving out through the courtyard into the narrow, twisting, tree-lined streets of Palma.

Drums and trumpets flourished into martial music. The beadle, voice of order and protocol, wearing a rich velvet robe and carrying the mace of authority, led the procession. Behind him the university rector strode with dignified elegance in a long, purple robe, splendidly embroidered in red and gold and trailing a long velvet train carried by a little page staggering under its heavy weight.

Crowds watched as they wound slowly and magnificently through the town and up the hill to the bishop's palace. Nearby, the great cathedral, like a majestic fortress, dominated the busy Bay of Palma.

In a few moments His Excellency appeared, radiant in a scarlet silken robe with ermine cape. He wore the tall white and gold tiara, crowning symbol of his office, and carried the golden staff of the Shepherd. Leading the procession, His Excellency was followed by attendants, the mayor, aldermen, visiting nobles, government officials and other prominent dignitaries.

Trumpets, drums, stringed instruments accompanied singing minstrels in rousing rhythmic hymns and marching songs. The people of Palma and their guests watched, filling the town square, the narrow streets, overhead balconies and fences. Some even perched precariously in trees.

Majorcans had only perfunctory interest in officials. What set their minds afire were the color, the emblems, the symbols of their faith, their history, their heritage, their hopes. History had dealt harshly with these people. Hundreds of years of Moorish persecution, oppression and violent desecration of all that was Christian were still—even after centuries of rebirth— vivid memories, keen, living and in a way personal. Majorcans were not fired by desires for revenge, however, but by the pride of Christian victory, by determination to keep what had been all but lost. Today's procession was an outward expression of gratitude, dedication and renewed enthusiasm for the faith that was their life. To eighteenth-century Majorcans, loyalty to the emblem of the cross superseded loyalty to a flag.

In 1229, James I of Aragón freed Majorca from Moorish occupation and dispersed the hordes of ruthless pirates and buccaneers whose stronghold of plunder and outrage had been the Bay of Palma.

Christianity, crushed and forced underground, had begun picking up the pieces. Rebuilding and rejuvenation were slow and difficult, but with liberation emerged not only the vivification and deepening of Christian faith but a poignant awareness of freedom.

Ramón Lull appealed to the Majorcan spirit. Born just six years after Majorcan liberation, this fiery nobleman had led a life of reckless adventure until his "conversion." Self-alienated from worldly pursuits, he had become equally daring and audacious as a defender of the faith—a brilliant scholar, educator, poet, philosopher, recluse and missionary.

At a time when intense hatreds were flaring into violence and atrocities, and indelible bitterness gnawed at souls on both sides, he had stood like a flaming sword between the cross and the crescent. Lull went into the heart of Islam Africa, lived with Moslems, learned their language, studied their books and succeeded in converting Arabs to Christianity. He hoped by physical contact, intellectual understanding and selfless love to close the gap of hundreds of years of anguish. He hoped, too, to tap the vast store of knowledge of mathematics, engineering, astronomy, chemistry, medicine and other sciences accumulated through Arab conquests of successive civilizations. He wanted to bring this knowledge home to Spanish schools and universities. In return, Islam's reward would be the

Christian faith. "Not to love is death and love is life,"[2] was the motto for which he lived and died. Above all, he longed to end the long-standing enmity between Arab and Spaniard. But Islam would not buy his plan. He did make hundreds of converts. He transported much of the knowledge which was to be inculcated in Spanish schools. But at the age of eighty-one, he was martyred. Upon these facts Serra would base his sermon.

―――――――――――

The procession's arrival at the church was announced by a flutter of drums and trumpeting finale. Each dignitary according to rank, tradition and protocol, was escorted to his place.

Magnificently baroque, the interior of the old church needed no adornment. Conscientious parishioners, however, had decorated the main altar and twenty-one side altars with brightly colored, fresh flowers. The walls were draped with silk brocade, and banners hung from the ceiling. Thousands of flickering candles illuminated the vast nave, casting weird shadows in darkened corners. Their light penetrated rolling clouds of incense and disseminated misty, eerie waves, moving across high, rose-colored, stained-glass windows.

Solemn high Mass began. The mesmeric pace of the ritual of that ancient, traditional ceremony, which daily reenacts the drama of salvation, was accentuated by the chanting of Majorca's finest choir. The officiating priest sang the Gospel in rhythmic, climactic tones; then it was time for the sermon.

Fr. Serra climbed the semicircular stairway leading to a small, cupular pulpit. All was quiet. In anticipa-

―――――――

2. Daniel-Rops, *Cathedral and Crusade*, p. 512.

tion, everyone looked toward the speaker. He was very small up there, his shoulders hardly clearing the missal stand. But the depth, strength and volume of his musical voice drew full attention. No one regarded stature, as all surrendered to that sonorous voice.

The sermon, Fr. Palóu said, was "dramatic and eloquent." We know it was one of Serra's finest. It won applause far and wide. Thirty years later, Fr. Palóu wrote that he had heard one of the professors remark: "This sermon is worthy of being printed in letters of gold."

We cannot record the words. They are lost to posterity. But sermons fit only a given time and circumstance. We can be certain, however, that Fr. Serra's words rang with his apostolic zeal, his dynamic personality, his profound simplicity.

This was the pinnacle of Serra's academic career. Open to him were greater honors—a bishopric, perhaps, or assignment as rector of the university, or as provincial superior of the Order of St. Francis.

But Fr. Serra was not born to accumulate honors, praise and high positions. He was foreordained for other goals. As the sun set on the ceremonies, this day would mark the climax of his achievements in the eastern hemisphere. Adventures he could neither plan nor conceive were soon to begin.

Home Is
a Seminary

The serene farming village of Petra lay about twenty-five miles inland from Palma. Most everyone was asleep that November night in 1713. But in the square, stone house at No. 6 Barracar Avenue, a light was burning.

Margarita Serra was in labor. This was not her first child. Since their marriage, Margarita Ferrer and Antonio Serra had had two children, a boy and a girl. Both had died in infancy. For nine long months Margarita had hoped and prayed that this time all would be well. Still, apprehension grew as the pains accelerated through the long, anxious hours.

Then at one o'clock in the morning, there was a cry, the unmistakable cry of an infant. The Serras had a boy! He seemed to be a normal baby, small, a bit on the frail side, but apparently healthy. Previous experience, however, had left sharp wounds.

The devout parents were keenly aware that this new fragile bit of life, too, could be snatched from them. Helpless before the dim intangible of Miguel's earthly survival, they took prudent precautions to assure his eternal joy as a baptized son of Christ. As soon as morning came, Antonio saw the padre and arranged for Baptism that very day, the 24th of November. The name was no problem. They would call him Miguel, as they had called their first son.

The simple baptism was brief and devout. Only relatives and a few close friends attended. The midwife led the modest procession to St. Peter's Church, with Miguel snuggled in her arms. The tiny babe was almost lost in the family heirloom dress, long, white, elaborately embroidered and trimmed with lace. Around all this finery was wrapped a clean wool blanket to keep him warm. The godparents walked behind, followed by the others. The godmother, Sebastian Serra, Antonio's sister, held the baby during the ceremony but returned him to the care of the midwife when they left the church. Antonio gave the priest some fruit for his trouble, then all returned to the Serra home. The midwife placed the baptized Miguel in his mother's arms with the words, "Ja'l vos tornam Cristai," ("I return him to you a Christian").[1] The little group sat around the living room, chatted a while, ate some cookies and drank a little wine or brandy. Then each guest offered a toast to the proud parents. "Congratulations! May God give you joy in him, and may he be a good boy."[2]

By now most everyone in the closely knit, little town of Petra knew that the Serras had a baby boy. What they could not know was that Miguel Serra was destined to be the Apostle of the holy Catholic faith—

1. Geiger, *op. cit.*, p. 6.
2. *Ibid.*

that living, motivating force of Majorcan life, history and tradition—on far western shores, in a land then practically unknown, a land called California.

Aligned with the other houses on Barracar Avenue, the Serra home stood flush with the narrow, cobbled street. Centuries old, the plain but sturdy, two-story house, built of stone, was a little roomier than some in the neighborhood, but in most respects typical of the farm houses of the area. In front a wide, arched doorway was entrance for the mule, the cart and the family. A square door to the left led to a corridor separating the cart shelter and the mule corral from the rest of the house. The living quarters, with cement floor and whitewashed walls, were clean, neat and immaculately scrubbed. The parlor was simply furnished with only a table, a couple of chairs, a bench and a chest for linens. The bedroom was just large enough for the bed and a small table. Opening from the living room, an alcove served as the kitchen. Consisting mostly of a wide, deep fireplace, it answered the purpose of a cook stove, light, heat and the center for family and friendly gatherings. In fact, except for the one small window above the door, the fireplace was the only source of light for that part of the house. Upstairs were another bedroom and a storage room.

Like most Majorcan families, the Serras farmed their own land. Ownership, established through a long line of ancestors, generated love of the land, loyalty, permanence and security.

Approximately in the center of Majorca, Petra was located on a fertile plateau. The soil was good, some of the best on the agricultural island. Life was gratifying, but it was rough. The people worked hard. A man's returns depended on his own initiative, his muscular ability to coax from the earth its maximum production and nature's response to his urging, to the rain and the sun and the renewal of spring. Farmers held no illusions, no soaring hopes, for well they knew that spring could be a benefactor or a tyrant. All had seen abundant crops smashed by an unseasonal storm or seared by drought. Majorcans were conditioned to hardship. They were stolid, patient, forbearing, and full of fun and grace.

Majorcans were not essentially Spanish. Extremely insular, they were a mixture of races and characteristics. Drawn together by similar problems and interests, free from status complexities and the sham of sophistication, they faced realities in mutual awareness. Life was simple. Their food, mostly produced on the farms, was plain but usually plentiful. Generally speaking, they were robust, vigorous people of good stature. They strode with a calm, natural grace and the dignity of a proud heritage, enhanced by the charm of a ready, friendly smile. And beneath the hardy physical exterior seethed a virile vivacity. Life was not dull.

Entertainment usually centered around the home or community. Naturally cheerful spirits could spontaneously burst into exhilaration of clear, musical song or exciting, fast-paced graceful dancing. Education was limited, but they were eager to learn.

Miguel was three when a sister, Juana María, born in January, 1716, joined the family group. The two little ones played and grew up together, but of Margarita and Antonio's five children, only these two survived. Another little girl, Martina María, was born four years later, but died very young.

We can look back and see that Miguel's character was being formed in the earliest years of his childhood. The priests at St. Bernardine's and St. Peter's were close family friends. They frequently visited at the

Serra home and Miguel saw them at Mass. At Margarita's knees he learned his prayers, and through her example, training, influence and love he acquired a deep and lasting love for the Blessed Mother. Both parents implicitly believed and taught their children that life was a gift of God and that it was the primary purpose of each individual to serve him. Theirs was the comforting security of total belief. They accepted their Catholicism as divine truth, complete, dependable, holy—won through sacrifice, blood and the cross. It was theirs to hold, to defend, to share.

Although neither Margarita nor Antonio could read or write, both held a high regard for education and were determined that their son should have every opportunity to learn. At an early age Miguel showed evident signs of being an exceptionally bright boy. Education at that time was available to almost any boy, with or without money if he had the will and the inclination to learn. Antonio needed a son to help on the farm. But his desire that Miguel should have the best educational and religious training superseded all selfish interests.

St. Bernardine's, called the pearl of all the churches of the province (excepting St. Francis of Palma) was only a block from Miguel's home. Smaller than St. Peter's, but with more delicate lines, it was truly a gem for a town of fifteen hundred to two thousand people.

Next to the church, the Franciscans had built a friary and school for boys. To live practically next door to so fine a school was most fortunate for Miguel. He quickly absorbed mathematics, Latin, reading, writing and religion in the friendly environment. From the first, the monks recognized in this boy a natural talent for music. They asked if he would like to join them in the choir, and almost before he could read, his pure, clear musical tones joined the monks in Divine Office and Gregorian chant.

After school and on vacations Miguel could help at home with the planting, cultivating and harvesting, and with caring for the animals. Under Antonio's direction and companionship, he witnessed nature's mysterious promise and fulfillment. The magical responsive cooperation of nature, man and the Creator would become a vital part of Miguel's inner being.

Among other things, he learned that fundamental to any type of farming operation were rich, deep soil, an abundant water supply and a favorable climate. This early orientation to the land and its practical applications would in later years prove indispensable to the attainment of his goals.

But Miguel's interests began to turn away from the soil. At fifteen, he decided to become a Franciscan. Too young for admission as a novice (the minimum age was sixteen), he decided to enter the preparatory study course. This meant leaving home. The nearest training school and Franciscan seminary were in Palma.

Consequently, one September day in 1729, Miguel, Margarita and Antonio left the family home in Petra, each poignantly aware that this was the first break. The pain of separation was to the Serra's, as to most sincerely religious families, sorrow mixed with joy. Over and above the parents' personal emotions was profound gratitude that their son had been chosen for so noble a calling in the service of God.

Historians say only that they "rode" to Palma. No one tells us by what means they "rode," but it would have been natural to hitch the family mule to the cart and jog along the hot, dry, dusty twenty-five miles of rough, narrow, winding roads.

As they approached the walled city, they could see the massive towers of Palma's Gothic cathedral looming majestically against the sky. The charming city of about thirty thousand people, sloped semicircularly from the mountains to the sparkling, blue bay. Besides the cathedral, Palma boasted of architecturally perfect "La Longa," the center of trade, La Almudiana, the Moorish castle, the bishop's palace, the College of Sapeinta, the Lullian University and sixty churches and chapels. Among the most beautiful of these were the church and monastery of St. Francis, founded in 1232. Here Miguel was to register. Their journey was completed. Miguel said good-bye to his parents, and Margarita and Antonio made their way slowly back to Petra.

Three months after his sixteenth birthday, Miguel made formal petition for admission to the Order. This meant a personal interview with the provincial superior. At last the day came. Miguel stood before Fray Antonio Perelló Marqués and saw an influential and distinguished leader—a gentle, brilliant, spiritual man. The provincial looked down at a very small boy. He was surely too small to be sixteen and certainly too weak and sickly for the strenuous training of the novitiate. Thinking of the boy's welfare and his own responsibilities for the entire group—and no doubt, suspicious of a lie concerning Miguel's age—the provincial refused admission.

This was a bitter blow to Miguel. Yet his disappointment was dulled somewhat by the inspiration of meeting this fine man. His determination was firmer than before to pursue his vocation. He asked friends to intercede for him. In time, they convinced the provincial that Miguel was indeed sixteen and that his eagerness and enthusiasm would compensate for his lack of physical strength.

On September 14, 1730, Miguel was invested with the long gray habit and hood of the Franciscan Order at the Convento Santa María de los Ángeles de Jesús. This small, unassuming monastery, with the long name, was ideally located for a novitiate, in a secluded spot in the silence of the woods outside the city's walls.

Miguel was still too short to reach the lectern and too weak for certain physical exercises. But it was a happy year and perhaps one of the most important in molding the man.

His freedom from certain chores gave him time to read. *The Chronicles of Our Seraphic Order,* the story of the lives of the saintly men who had founded the order, became a part of him. He knew them as living friends. He told his fellow students of their colorful episodes, their hopes, their characters and the love that motivated all their actions: to seek nothing from this world, to trust all to God and to convert the whole world to the teaching of Christ. He longed to be like them. These were not the vain musings of youth. They were fundamental to his becoming the man God had destined him to be.

After one more year of self-sacrifice and rigorous discipline, on September 15, 1731, Miguel with his fellow novices knelt before their provincial and made the vows of poverty, chastity and obedience. Each had the privilege of taking a name other than his own. Miguel chose the name of the jolly extrovert, Junípero, "out of devotion to this holy companion of St. Francis, his deeds of holy simplicity and supernatural charm."[3] Often in later years, he told his dear friend Fr. Palóu, "All good things came to me with profession," and he renewed his vows each year. "With my profession I

---

3. G. W. James, *Palóu's Life of Junípero Serra,* p. 3.

gained health and strength and grew to medium size, for which I give infinite thanks to God."[4]

Now that he was a Franciscan, Fray Junípero Serra would have to study six more years before he could be ordained a priest. He was moved back to Convento de San Francisco, where he had registered two years before. Here he delved into the intensive study of philosophy and theology. The Latin classics and Scriptures were etched into his memory, ready and alive to be quoted in sermons throughout his life.

He reached for wisdom and learning as ladders to truth and to God. The Book of Wisdom well expresses Serra's serious love of books: "I prayed and prudence was given to me; I pleaded and the spirit of Wisdom came to me...the riches I do not hide away. For to me she is an unfailing treasure; those who gain this treasure win the friendship of God."[5]

His reputation as an earnest student and remarkably fine speaker was spreading outside monastery walls. The title of doctor of philosophy earned for him a position of university professor, and parish priests from other Majorcan cities were asking him to preach on special feast days.

In Serra's time the sermon was more than a homily. There was no television, no radio, very little outside entertainment. The sermon was the center of information and sometimes of news. The spoken word was all important. People listened reflectively: evaluating, dissecting, appraising. Serra's sermons electrified his audiences with enchanting bits of science, history, anecdotes and Scotus philosophy. He understood his fellow Majorcans, and his profound love for them reached

---

4. *Ibid.*
5. Wisdom 7:7-14.

into their souls, drawing them closer to friendship with the saints, the Blessed Mother and our Lord.

In the winter of 1737, he was ordained. Father Junípero Serra would be a priest forever. In the eight years since the frail boy had come with Margarita and Antonio from the farm in Petra to Palma he had grown physically, spiritually and intellectually. He had made close friends in the monastery.

He spent twelve more busy years in Palma—preaching, training young aspirants for the priesthood, and teaching as a professor at the Lullian University. But in 1749, the heralded Ramón speaker whose words "should be printed in letters of gold" would spurn honors for the greater love of the cross.

"Home is the seminary of all other institutions."[6] Margarita and Antonio had done their work well. Their exemplary counsel "to serve God alone" and St. Francis' code: "Glory only in the Cross of Christ" had piloted the boy to manhood and the man to the top of religious and scholastic service in his native Majorca. But the walls of security and established culture were not to hold this bold spirit. From his earliest years the cross had been the symbol of impassioned love that embraced all humanity, its sufferings, its needs, its wants. Now the spark of fragile life that had glowed on Barracar Avenue one November night, thirty-six years before, burned in a magnanimous love that transcended native boundaries, culture and fixed customs. It was reaching out to a multitude of souls living in darkness, entangled in ignorance and despair. Serra, the priest, the professor, the apostle, would bring to those souls new ways to live, new ways to think, and the hope and light of Truth.

---

6. E. H. Chapin.

New Worlds
for Old

A few words spoken in confidence, a personal letter intercepted, a bit of private conversation overheard, and a rumor starts—even in monastic halls. Fr. Serra presumed that all he had told of his missionary aspirations was securely locked in the confidence of his superior. But superiors have assistants and walls have ears. How or from what source secretive whisperings grew into rumors—no one knows.

But one day there was a knock on Fr. Palóu's cell door. His friend, Fr. Raphael Verger, had news. One of their own priests, someone right here at St. Francis', was going to the New World as a missionary. No. He didn't know who.

Dazzled, but managing to suppress his excitement, Fr. Palóu dismissed his friend as quickly as courtesy allowed and went into a reverie. At first it seemed impossible. If it were true, who was this intrepid priest who dared challenge the thirty-six year old ban? Palóu's concern reached beyond curiosity or politics. Since seminary days he had discouraged the compelling desire within him to become involved in missionary work. How many other Majorcan vocations had been alienated by this political tyranny? Time generates changes. Palóu's hopes flared anew. How could he reach the one whose daring exceeded custom? Two applications could have a double impact. Answers did not come to calm his turmoil and he automatically turned to work and prayer.

Days passed. Then, another knock. Fr. Serra, his closest friend, wanted a few words with him. The two had first met as student and professor, but despite Serra's seniority, their friendship had ripened into an indissoluble union of understanding and mutual affection. Palóu promptly disclosed Verger's news and his own secret ambitions. It was a poignant moment for the two men as they looked at each other in profound comprehension.

"The rumor is true. I am the one," Serra said, then added, "Just now I resolved to invite you to go along on this journey; ever since I resolved to go, in my heart I felt an inclination to speak to you, as I was led to believe you were interested."[1] If this was a great moment between the two friends who were united in the presence of Christ and who regarded prayer as real as the sunrise and the morning dew, then it was also a page of history for the New World. As a team, they would work in mutual commitment to the fulfillment of their common, complex goal.

Both agreed that secrecy was essential to the consummation of their project. Already they had verification that a word or sign could spark a proliferation of

1. James, *op. cit.*, p. 7.

rumors that might destroy their hopes before they were given a chance to materialize.

Serra set the wheels in motion. All details regarding the foreign missions were handled by a central governmental agency in Madrid. He wrote Fray Matías de Velasco, Commissary General of the Indies, requesting missionary assignment for Palóu and himself. He purposely made no territorial specifications. At that time, Franciscans were active in Mexico, Peru, the Philippines and all other lands under Spanish domain.

His letter arrived in Madrid at a propitious moment. Two commissaries from Mexico had just arrived for the specific purpose of selecting missionaries for the New World. Fr. Velasco, nevertheless, sent a cold, deliberate letter to Serra, stating that all quotas were filled and that, in fact, sixty-three missionaries were standing by in Cádiz, waiting for ships to take them across the Atlantic.

Serra knew that intervals between Atlantic sailings were from six months to a year and regarded Velasco's letter as a rejection. One slight ray of hope, however, left some encouragement. Velasco had added that should vacancies occur, he would think of them.

The promise was vague and Serra, a man of action, wrote the apostolic missionary preparatory college on the mainland, requesting application for admission for two.

Letters traveled slowly and Serra had work to do. Lent began on February 19. It was the custom for parish priests to invite a special guest speaker for the penitential sermons and instructions. Petra invited Serra. As Serra accepted this unexpected opportunity, he was deeply grateful for this generous gift in the divine drama, this last visit to his home town before leaving this part of the world forever. The old Franciscan monastery of San Bernardino, endeared by happy childhood memories, was his home through those delightful days in Petra.

In the meantime, things were happening in Madrid. Five of the prospective missionaries who had been waiting in Cádiz defected. Political pressure may have penetrated high places. In any case, the commission agreed to accept Serra's and Palóu's applications. After deliberate consideration—no doubt pressed by Mexico's demands for priests and by drop-outs from the continent—the Spanish commissary released the outdated Majorcan ban and sent assignment papers to both priests for missionary work in New Spain. But neither Palóu nor Serra received the papers.

The commissar's messenger delivered them to the monastery, but for reasons of his own, the superior tucked them away in his desk. This is somewhat difficult to understand. No doubt, his was an impulsive act, goaded by the barren hope that his two top men might become discouraged and give up the plan. Understandably, too, he must have feared that once the news was out that the ban had been lifted, a rash of requests for missionary work would leave serious vacancies in his well-organized establishment. After an unreasonable period of frustration in both Palma and Madrid, the commissary, suspecting foul play, tried again. This time he gave explicit orders to place the papers personally in the hands of either Palóu or Serra. No one else!

Palm Sunday tingled with the sparkling spring beauty of a glorious Mediterranean morning. Palóu, deep in meditation, was walking to the chapel for the blessing of the palms when suddenly someone rushed up to him excitedly chattering a confusion of words, whose purport was "a personal messenger is here with important papers for you."[2]

Palóu, at long last, went to the superior with the assignments in his hand. Defeated in his futile intrigue, the superior gave permission, and Palóu immediately left for Petra.

Later, when he wrote the biography of Serra, Palóu (who never refers to himself) says of Serra that it was "for him a source of greater joy and happiness than if he had received a royal decree naming him to some bishopric."[3]

At St. Bernardine's that night, the lights burned late as the two friends discussed plans. Since no imminent trans-Atlantic sailing was scheduled, there was time for Serra to complete his mission at Petra. Palóu would take care of the necessary details. He sent their acceptances to the commissary, arranged for replacements and other affairs pertinent to leaving St. Francis, and made reservations for transportation to Cádiz, the official port of departure and rendezvous for missionaries to the New World. Both agreed it was still best not to discuss their plans with those not involved.

It would be a sacrifice not to share his elation with his parents, but he sensed that the shock would be too much if they were aware that this farewell embrace would be his last good-bye. Neither of the missionaries wanted emotional demonstrations nor adulation. They wanted only to slip quietly from the scene and get on with the work to be done.

Established customs rarely changed in that part of the world. As they had on every Tuesday morning after Easter for hundreds of years, most everyone in Petra assembled at St. Peter's for the final ceremonies that

---

2. *Ibid.*
3. *Ibid.*

completed the lenten and Easter observances. They loved Serra because he was one of Petra's sons and because, as visiting priest on recurring occasions, he had re-enkindled their professed faith with new hope and love.

Serra led the traditional procession as all solemnly sang, prayed and marched up the zig-zag path to the shrine of Mare de Bon Any, atop the hill. Here the faithful came all through the year to pray for the recovery of a loved one or the success of crops; expectant mothers would pray to St. Anne, the mother of the Blessed Mother of Jesus. Without doubt Margarita had come here thirty-five years before to pray for the physical and spiritual welfare of her child. Now, Margarita, seventy, and Antonio, seventy-three, were not too feeble to make the trip.

After the ceremonies, as a gesture of appreciation to the visiting priest, each pilgrim knelt and kissed Serra's hand. These were his people—his schoolmates, their wives, their children, his neighbors, his relatives. They could not know that as he looked affectionately into the eyes of each, their dear friend and priest was saying good-bye to them forever.

From the hilltop shrine, this beautiful April morning, Serra could view a panorama of his native Majorca. Rich, green valleys and neat, church-spired villages nestled among the mountains—mountains stretching out in every direction, yet always bending to the sea. Directly below was Petra: her square stone houses set stolidly in rows forming a kind of rectangle with St. Peter's bulky, square tower rising protectively at one end and at the other, St. Bernardine's slender, artistic spire pointing toward heaven. Softening the severity of stone, were shade and fruit trees spreading their branches, gardens flashing color, vineyards sprouting new, brownish-green leaves. Windmills turned lazily in the soft Mediterranean breeze and livestock grazed contentedly in lush meadows. Fenced off in neat declaration of ownership, fields flushed the bright new-green of spring. Beyond was the sea, the unknown, but from this foundation-rock of firm, deeply rooted faith would emanate new hope, new vision, new civilizations of people utterly different, with whom Serra would relate even more intimately than he had with his own.

When Margarita and Antonio had left Miguel at Palma twenty years before, their renunciation had been final. Without benefit of theological reasoning, they had accepted the pain of separation with the true devotion of Catholic parents. But they had had the implied consolation, the comforting certainty that Majorcan priests conventionally remained in Majorca and that Majorcan conventions endured. Change was unthinkable. He belonged to Majorca, to them. He would visit them periodically.

And Serra *had visited* them. How he must have cherished those precious moments, crowded with nostalgia: his mother's understanding, kindly precautions; his father's practical, sound advice, the unemotional but tenacious trust and affection between father and son, and the wisdom imparted in the field and at home.

At one point Antonio had become seriously ill and Miguel had been called home. Not expecting to recover, Antonio had said to his son, "Miguel, I ask but one thing of you. That is to be a true and faithful Franciscan."[4] Today, no doubt, those words resounded in Serra's mind as the last poignant moments passed. His parents bid, "Adios, Deo to quart de perill," ("Goodbye, may God protect you from all danger").

---

4. Geiger, *op. cit.*, p. 29.

Then Serra rode the twenty-five miles back to Palma.

Travel wasn't easy in 1749. The first scheduled sailing from Palma direct to Cádiz was months away. In order to save time, they had booked passage on a small English freighter, due to sail to Málaga in five days.

By now everyone at St. Francis' was alerted that Serra and Palóu were leaving. The farewells were tender, sincere and prayerful.

On the Sunday after Easter, the little ship hoisted the English flag, set sail and slipped away, leaving the familiar scenes of Palma and the mountains of Majorca far behind. It had been a busy and emotional week for the two missionaries. They looked forward to a few weeks of rest at sea.

But this was not to be. It seems they were the only passengers aboard. The captain turned out to be an argumentative, bullying bigot. He delighted in loud, controversial disputations and jubilantly pounced on the two unsuspecting "Spanish" priests as fair prey. Armed with the minimal primary-school compulsory catechetical instruction, he presumed to propound at length on all theological subjects. He may have been suffering from a sharp hatred of everything Spanish and Catholic. Feelings between England and Spain were extremely tense at that time. At any rate, his virulence and violence grew. Palóu's admonition that Serra was an eminent and famous doctor of theology and philosophy only fanned his passion, and Serra's reluctance to argue added fuel to his infuriated ego. One night Serra awoke to find this madman at his throat with a knife. Fortunately, however, the captain's anger cooled enough for him to stalk away, swearing profusely.

Málaga was a welcome port. After three days' lay-over, they boarded another ship, and after five days of sailing, entered the bustling harbor of Cádiz.

Cádiz is said to be the oldest city in the world. Its name has remained unchanged for over three thousand years. In 1749, it was one of the busiest, most dissolute and most cosmopolitan centers of the world. Defended by the sea on one side and by massive Roman and Moorish walls inland, this key port of Mediterranean power had been an age-old focal point of nationalistic bitterness and wars—ancient wars for supremacy in the Mediterranean, then Moorish domination and wars of freedom, wars with England, wars with France. The age of discovery and expansion had made it the gate-way to New Spain. Conquistadors, traders, adventurers, soldiers and missionaries departed from the port of Cádiz for New Spain, and white sails entered the secluded harbor with silver, gold, tobacco, new and strange vegetables and fruits. A thousand ships lay at anchor when Serra's boat slipped unnoticed into the bay. Warships, freighters, fishing boats, ships bound for the Orient to bring back spices and silks, ships that plied the Mediterranean ports.... Built on a long, narrow strip of land, the "white city" of square, flat-roofed buildings lay massed against an azure sea.

In the midst of this center of commerce and crime, power and intrigue, stood the lovely church and monastery of St. Francis, where missionary priests from all the provinces of Spain congregated, waiting for sailing orders. When Frs. Serra and Palóu reported to Fray Pedro Pérez de Mezquía, who was in charge of assignments, they learned that many Spanish priests had defected. Quotas waited to be filled. Fr. Serra assured Mezquía that there was no shortage of aspirants in Majorca. The ban had been lifted and the rush was on, just as the superior of St. Francis had feared. Many of Serra's friends at St. Francis' had confided to Serra their eagerness for missionary work. Credentials were sent to Frs. Juan Crespí and Guillermo Vicens, as well as to the news-bearer, Fr. Raphael Verger.

The red tape associated with missionary assignments might be compared to present-day government bureaucracy. Though emissaries of the Catholic Church, all missionaries were agents of the State. All missionary work was carried out under government auspices. Transportation and physical support of each missionary were the responsibility of the king. Cumbrous as the arrangement was, it did provide economic and military aid to the missionary movement, and without it progress in newly discovered lands would have been impossible. Paradoxically, however, this entanglement of Church and State eventually led to the collapse of the missions.

Serra and Palóu were delayed four months in Cádiz. Serra took this opportunity to write to his parents. He addressed the letter to a priest at St. Bernardine's, asking him to read it to them. It was direct and without sentimentality, but from it emanated the same mutual faith that had penetrated their lives. He knew that his parents would understand that this was God's will for him and that they would not want him to turn back. He must always go forward, as his vocation directed.

To Fr. Francesch, the priest at St. Bernardine's, he wrote: "Words cannot express the feelings of affection that overwhelm me, for those who I know are going through a great sorrow. I wish I could give them some of the happiness that is mine, and I feel they would urge me to go ahead and never to turn back. Nothing less than the love of God has led me to leave them."

Delays eventually come to an end. Around September 1, they were off again. Our friends, with eighteen other Franciscans and seven Dominicans, boarded the *Villasota*, alias *Nuestra Señora de Guadalupe*. (All Spanish ships seemed to bear two names.) It was one of the finest ships that plied the Atlantic, but when we look at the replicas of such top-heavy vessels, we are astounded that forty passengers, plus the crew could have survived in them.

At the mercy of vacillating winds, the *Villasota* bobbed, rolled and glided south and north, but made a gradual semi-controlled progression westward. Serra said Mass when possible, but was compelled to wait for calm seas, when there was no danger of spilling the precious Blood. Day and night he wore on his breast the wooden cross, symbol of love. He offered his own inconveniences in devotion to Christ.

The water supply gave out before the middle of October. No chocolate for breakfast, the equivalent of no coffee in our time. They made it to San Juan, Puerto Rico, with no disaster and replenished the supply of water. Serra, in characteristic zeal, posted announcements for a mission. There was enthusiastic response to the summons of the zealous missionary with the clear, musical voice.

After eighteen days in Puerto Rico, the *Villasota*, well-stocked with fruits and supplies, left in its wake renewed hope and peace.

Plenty to eat, pleasant seas, all was going smoothly. Then, only one day from their destination, Vera Cruz, a terrifying storm hit with the ferocity of a hurricane. Mast-high waves, torrential rains and savage winds rolled, tossed and dipped the uncontrollable ship. Disaster seemed certain. The crew mutinied.

Serra remained calm. He called together the missionaries of both orders and proposed a novena of prayer to St. Barbara. Before the nine days were up, the storm subsided. The valiant little ship was battered and shaken, but she had proven her sea-worthiness. She rallied and resumed her course. On December 6, the small vessel proudly entered the harbor of Vera Cruz, Mexico.

A Mass of thanksgiving was offered soon after disembarking. Then the missionaries sought transportation from the eastern seaport to Mexico City, 270 miles inland.

There was little choice. Most of the new arrivals followed the customary means of travel: horseback or muleback. Serra chose to walk. An Andalusian priest, whose name has been lost in the oblivion of history, accompanied Serra. Palóu rode because he had become ill at sea.

Following El Camino Real, the King's Highway, which was no more than a mule trail, they climbed from sea level to mountain heights over seven thousand feet in altitude. They trekked past volcanoes and lakes, across dry plains, and through tropical jungles. They forded swollen rivers. Mysterious help came to them at crucial times. Several incidents, well known to history, indicate the intervention of the supernatural. This account, however, is neither a theological discussion nor a proof of sanctity. Suffice it to mention that food, shelter and guidance appeared at crucial moments in regions where no man nor dwelling was thought to exist.

They made the crossing safely and in good health except for one incident. Serra was bitten in the leg by a venomous tropical insect, the *zancudo*. The bite left a painful sting, followed by severe swelling and itching.

In his sleep, Serra must have scratched it, for it became infected, leaving a permanent ulcerous condition that caused serious suffering the rest of his life.

When Serra arrived at the College of San Fernando in Mexico City, the long, arduous journey from Palma was completed.

Although still known as the New Spain, Mexico had been a thriving province for more than two hundred years. Great cathedrals, magnificent churches filled with fine works of art, schools, hospitals, colleges as fine as any in Europe, and the renowned shrine of Our Lady of Guadalupe, all testified to the ambitious program and illimitable energy of those who had come to the New World. Pacific seaports flourished. Ships loaded with supplies and treasures from China and the Philippines plied a busy and lucrative trade. But outlying areas were still inhabited by wild native peoples. Spain, the king and the Church were dedicated to the civilization, not the extermination of these Indians.

San Fernando College was the training school and general headquarters for preparing priests for the task. Here they equipped themselves with some of the spiritual and physical stamina required in the vigorous life, hardships and deprivations of missionary work. They learned dialects, that they might speak to the native Americans in the tongue natural to them. They learned Indian habits and customs. In this framework they would approach them as friends and reach out to them in understanding, coming not as conquerors but as ambassadors of the love of Christ.

Serra had left his titles and his honors in Palma. Now, simply as Fr. Junípero, he asked to be admitted to the training courses as a novice. It was his wish to strengthen himself both physically and spiritually for the task ahead. The thirty-six year old Lullian doctor of theology submitted freely, enthusiastically and with fresh zeal to the confinement and conformity of novice-ship.

After five months of training, he was given an assignment to missionary work.

The Builder

Sierra Gorda, northeast of Mexico City, was one of those remote sections of the Spanish New World which after two hundred years of conquest still presented problems. The nature of the land itself seemingly argued against progress and easy solutions. Wild and wooded, this mountainous region teemed with mountain lions, coyotes, deer, countless varieties of venomous snakes, rare, brightly colored tropical birds and myriads of flying and crawling insects. It was rugged, rebellious and full of contrasts: high peaks and deep canyons; intense, humid, oppressive heat and bitter, stinging cold; tempestuous storms that suddenly turned gentle streams into raging torrents, and serene, moonlit evenings, singing with cicadas.

Scattered between the folds of the overshadowing mountains were comparatively fertile valleys, where the Pame Indians scratched the earth, planted and harvested maize corn.

Bronze-skinned, with thick, flat features and coarse, black hair, the Pames of Sierra Gorda were considered more gentle than their cousins who lived to the north, around Sonora. But hunger or an angry mood could flare into a wild raid on a neighboring village, with burning, looting and murdering.

Spasmodic attempts had been made to bring civilizing and christianizing influences to the Pames. In the early days of Spanish occupation, Augustinian monks had penetrated the area, brought seeds, taught the rudiments of cultivation and made some progress toward christianizing the natives. Not until 1740 did the Pames become the responsibility of the Franciscans. Building and expansion in the immense new continent had always demanded more trained men than were available. Still, the Franciscans tried to respond to every call, by spreading thin, turning older provinces over to parish priests and constantly calling for more volunteers from Spain.

Sierra Gorda was a mosquito-infested area. Malaria, smallpox, tuberculosis and dysentery had claimed the lives of many missionaries. In 1744, ten Franciscans established five missions in Sierra Gorda. Four thousand Indians lived at the missions, worked in the fields and were learning skills and Christian ways, when tragedy struck again. Three of the fathers died in a single month, another soon after. With almost half of the little force gone and the others ill, the project was abandoned.

Again, in 1750, the guardian of San Fernando called for volunteers for Sierra Gorda. To Serra the call meant that everything was falling into place. Now, less than a year after arriving in the New World, he had completed his San Fernando training. This opportunity for missionary work was what he had been waiting for. At the meeting volunteers were asked for. Eagerly, Serra's voice was heard above the rest. "Here I am. Send me."[1] Secretly, the San Fernando officials had hoped to keep this talented speaker and distinguished theologian in the Mexico City area. Outlying parishes, near and far, constantly demanded intelligent, well-educated speakers from San Fernando. But Serra left no doubt in the minds of his superiors that his sole purpose in coming to the New World had been missionary service. His good friends and fellow Majorcans, Frs. Palóu and Crespí, joined Serra as volunteers for Sierra Gorda. All together, ten made up the group—two for each mission.

A few Christian Indian interpreters and guides, a soldier, riding horses and pack mules came down to Mexico City to lead them over the two-hundred-mile winding, dusty, mountainous trail. Most of the missionaries rode, but Serra and Palóu chose to walk. At an average of fifteen miles a day, with occasional rests, they made the trip in sixteen days.

Home for Serra and Palóu was the dismal, dilapidated wreck of Jalpan, the central mission of the Sierra Gorda group. The natives greeted them joyously, but there was little lasting evidence of previous missionary endeavors.

Hanging as uncertainly as its Christian influences, the little settlement was perched along the hillsides above the Rio de Jalpan. The stream was placid enough in June, but most anytime a sudden storm could turn it into a rampaging and flooding torrent. A few large sabinto trees, growing along the river banks, offered shade. On a flat area, scraped off for the purpose, stood the simple, run-down, adobe church, a friary and a few cane-thatched shacks, all dilapidated and grimy.

---

1. Geiger, *op. cit.*, p. 100.

Enthusiastically and vigorously, the two young priests met the challenge of their new vocation. We speak of "young" priests here, remembering that when Serra was thinking of leaving the university, he was concerned about being too old. I feel confident that he left in Majorca the eminence and the responsibilities that bow the shoulders down with care.

As in any era, one's age depends not so much on the number of years he has lived, as upon his physical condition, activity and mental outlook. Serra was a young, healthy, vigorous thirty-six. The renewal of noviceship, and the hope of starting a new vocation undoubtedly conditioned him to start his new work with the same eagerness and youthful exuberance as a newly ordained priest. The fact that his best friends, Crespí and Palóu, were former pupils, would lead us to assume that Serra stayed young in thought and spirit.

The first project was to learn the Pame language. Every Indian dialect was different. Those studied at San Fernando no doubt helped, but Pames spoke something else, and communication came first. The missionaries learned to speak the dialect, and translated the catechism, liturgy and other prayers into Pame. Then they settled on a plan of community life.

At sunrise and sunset the mission bells rang out, calling everyone to the church. Together, they prayed the Mass and followed other devotions, then there was a brief instruction on Christian doctrine. This was carried out one day in Pame, the next day in Spanish. By learning Spanish, the natives enlarged their sphere of communication and could become an integral part of the country.

Serra's sense of the dramatic, his imagination and sense of humor helped him to reach the mind of the Indian. To explain abstract ideas, he would dramatize, motivate, encourage, warn and caution by simple application to everyday life and problems. And the intimate scenes of our Lord's life and that of his Blessed Mother came alive through pageantry, which the natives themselves could act out. By costume, live figures and the spoken word, the reality and spirit of the incarnation, nativity, resurrection, ascension and other biblical scenes were brought into relationship with their own lives. Many of these customs are still followed in South America and Mexico.

The Pames learned not only about God, but also how to live more productive lives. Through their contact with the Moors, the Spaniards, especially Majorcans, had advanced in the study of soils, irrigation practices and other important farming procedures. This knowledge the missionaries handed on to the natives of New Spain. They gave them seed and improved varieties of corn, beans, squash and sugar cane plants. They designed and built irrigation and drainage systems. All farming and other activity was on a communal basis. Food and other necessities were distributed according to needs.

Anticipating the day when the Pames would be integrated into a mixed society, the padres taught them business methods—how to buy, sell, bargain and choose the best outlet for their wares and how to distribute the proceeds. The latter was wisely done under the supervision and guidance of the padres, who made certain that all were treated fairly and that a reserve supply was held back against possible crop failure.

From the proceeds of the crops, Serra bought oxen, cows, bulls, mules, pigs, goats and implements for cultivation and harvesting. Both Serra and Palóu worked in the fields beside the natives. It soon became evident that Palóu had a special organizational ability, which

made him an efficient ranch manager. He appointed
the most dependable Indians as foremen, while he himself would supervise and oversee the projects. Although
the land, work and production were on a community
basis, the missionaries encouraged private enterprise.
Indians who showed special perseverance were given a
piece of land of their own, along with a yoke of oxen,
some livestock and seed. Others were rewarded according to their individual merits with blankets, clothing
and trinkets.

Religiously the Pames were growing, too. They enthusiastically responded to the little plays, pantomimes
and processions. That the basic truths were penetrating
was manifested by the regularity with which increasing
numbers received the sacraments. But they needed a
church, not just a shelter—a church where people could
meet and hold religious exercises; one that through its
beauty would give honor to God and inspiration to his
people.

To Serra a church was the consecrated space in that
particular locale where God takes up his presence,
where his divine Son is really present in the Blessed
Sacrament, and where, through this presence, the
earthly and heavenly spheres meet and fuse. It was a
temple of liturgical theology represented in stone,
wood, glass, art and music. It was the outward expression of love and unity, where each individual joins with
the community as a unified parish, with the Church as
a whole and with the entire world, in worship, praise
and glorification of Almighty God. And it should repre-
sent the worshipers' ultimate in workmanship and art.

The beautiful edifice in Jalpan stands as a gemlike
prototype of those ideals and as a lasting monument to
Serra's instincts for building, his artistic good taste and
most of all, his loving leadership, hard work and perse-

verance. There is no doubt that he hired an architect and professional masons, but much of the actual labor was done by the Indians, with Serra working at their side.

When the decision and plans were firm, Serra asked an Indian boy to ring the bells. Loud and clear, their call penetrated the entire area, summoning the Indians to assemble. They listened attentively as the padre told them how they could build a church, their own church, big enough for all the people—a beautiful church, one that would give just glory and joy to God.

Flattered that the padre would be interested in building a fine church in their Jalpan, the Indians enthusiastically volunteered to work on the project. It took seven years of hard work to complete. Serra wisely allowed the Indians to work on the church only when they were not needed in the fields. They worked as apprentices to the hired masons and learned and took pride in the skills of carpentry, iron-working, painting and stone masonry.

The women did their part too. Their knitting, weaving and stocking-making had been perfected to the point of building up a trade with other communities. They bought cotton from the outside, spun it and wove it into blankets, clothing and other articles, which they sold. The money from this trade, they used to pay the hired masons. When the church was finished they owed nothing; in fact, due to outside donations, there was a reserve in the treasury.

Built of yellowish-brown stone found nearby, the church is fifty-three yards long and eleven yards wide, with a high-vaulted ceiling and adjacent sacristy and chapel. A ninety-foot tower, with rounded openings for the bells, supports a five-foot ornamental iron cross. Reminiscent of the Majorcan-Moorish influence, the windows are Arabic in style; otherwise, the design is classic. The facade is beautifully decorated with statues and symbolic vines and wheat, all exquisitely and delicately blended into a delightful pattern. Today the church at Jalpan stands much as it was when finished over two hundred years ago: Spanish charm perpetuating the art, the ideals, the dreams of Fr. Junípero Serra.

The four other missions, under the leadership of Serra as president, were developing in varying degrees along the same lines as Jalpan. Each had built a church, but none compared in beauty and elaboration with Santiago de Jalpan. Many of the natives now owned their land and were independent farmers; others were sufficiently skilled to become independent; the granaries were filled; Spanish settlers were coming in and the Indians were becoming a civilized integral part of the growing area. Small Christian towns were springing up in the little valleys and, as in Majorca, their days were regulated by the sound of bells.

But they had their problems. Though the groundwork of establishing Sierra Gorda missions had previously been done, the three Majorcans had tasted their first rigors of missionary life and tested their capacity for self-abnegation and control. While most of the Indians were friendly and cooperative, among them were individuals behind whose silent, stoical exterior lurked hate and distrust. Violence was a constant threat, and on one occasion Serra narrowly escaped assassination. Hunger, filth, stench, sickness, death and the moodiness of tough Indians were a way of life. Only a steadfast and profound faith sustained the missionaries. Yet, avidly, Serra and his companions, with characteristic detachment and renunciation of human comforts, accepted and offered all these things and more in union with the cross of Christ for the salvation of the souls they had come to teach and direct.

He would "Always go forward; never turn back."[2] These words, written to his parents from Cádiz, formulated the firm intention from which he would never deviate, the motto he would follow indefatigably to the end.

The eight years at Sierra Gorda had been fruitful. The missionaries had followed in principle the missionary system established in New Spain two hundred years before, and the same plan would govern their future endeavors.

The work had been wrought with anguish, frustration and uncertainty, but there were rewards, the greatest of which was the affectionate response of many of the Indians to Serra's love. With clarity and patience he had taught about the purpose of life here on earth and the hope of eternal salvation. Through active participation in the realities and the ritual of the liturgy, the Indians had learned basic truths, prayers and the importance of honesty, charity and monogamy. Through the graces of Baptism, Confirmation and the other sacraments, the Holy Spirit had penetrated their souls, endowing many with a deep faith that would live on through successive generations.

A mutual love had developed between the padre, who had suffered, lived and worked with them, and his faithful native friends. But on September 26, 1758, Serra was called back to San Fernando and regretfully left Sierra Gorda behind. However, when Serra learned what plans they had for him, he was electrified. The viceroy had asked for four of San Fernando's top missionaries to go to San Sabá, the Apache country in Texas, where martyrdom was almost a certainty.

---

2. A. Tibesar, *Writings of Junípero Serra,* Vol. I, p. 3.

In the early months of 1758, the Comanches had staged a murderous raid on the San Sabá Mission, brutally killing and mutilating the priests and practically annihilating the settlement. The viceroy had decided that the raiders should not go unpunished. But the military expedition sent to punish the Comanches was defeated and mercilessly run out of the territory. This discouraged further plans and the whole project bogged down in confusion. It was a severe blow to Serra.

From 1758 to 1767, Serra's headquarters were the College of San Fernando in Mexico City, where he was on call for short missions, novenas and special sermons in other parts of Mexico. Once again the eloquent speaker charmed congregations with his clear, musical voice, his lively wit, ready smile, and fresh wisdom that reached into hearts with love and understanding. A less humble man would have accepted the unsolicited praise, flattery and adulation and comfortably settled down in an aura of eminence and fame. But in the New World, as in Majorca, Serra rejected popularity and acclaim. He obeyed the orders of his superior and served diligently on all assignments, but he accepted them as training in self-discipline, and spent his free time in prayer and austerities. He ate sparingly, and except for a brief afternoon siesta, slept only four hours, spending the rest of the night in prayer and meditation. Between assignments, when in residence at the college, he tenaciously followed the stringent rules for novices and training priests, and devoutly joined in the community prayers and liturgical exercises, growing in divine grace and the simplicity of love.

Bells
for Alta

"Yo el Rey," "I am the King." With this impressive statement Carlos III, King of Spain, sent a sealed, secret order to all the viceroys in his realm early in the year 1767. It was one of the extraordinary efforts of history, demanding ingenious measures of secrecy, planning and timing. Travel schedules for all personal couriers were so arranged as to assure that each royal document would be delivered into the hands of every viceroy in each province of the vast empire at approximately the same time, well ahead of the critical date, June 24. Anyone who opened the document before that date could be punished by death.

On the morning of June 24, Marqués de Croix, viceroy of New Spain, did as all deputies on the continent and in the other parts of the New World. He opened the document and read words that shook the world. All Jesuits were to be banished from Spanish soil! He, the viceroy, was thereby appointed agent, and

was so ordered, in the name of the king, to arrest and
deport to the Papal States every Jesuit then in New
Spain. Should one remain in the territory on comple-
tion of the embarkation, though he be incapacitated, ill
or dying, the viceroy would be put to death. No expla-
nations, no reasons were given for this rare, autocratic
use of monarchical power over a religious order. For
the more than six thousand popularly esteemed men,
many of whom were of the highest intelligence and
personal character in Spain, there would be no recourse, no trial. Discussion, questioning, irresolution
would be subject to the death penalty. Obedience must
be swift and absolute.

New Spain received the shock of this despotic measure with gravity. Religious orders had given spirit and
purpose to the growth, expansion and development of
the New World. For almost three hundred years, the
zealous Jesuits had courageously and compassionately
worked with the natives and settlers, disregarding pain,
hunger, disease and death. They had explored the wildest regions; established missions in barbarous lands;
built colleges, schools, seminaries and magnificent
churches. They had brought knowledge, culture and
Christianity to the New World.

Why? The unspoken question was on everyone's
mind. Carlos refused to tell his reasons, but "kept
[them] in his royal heart."[1]

Regardless of opinion, submission to the royal decree was imperative. As Tennyson later observed of
other despotic decrees: "Theirs not to make reply,
Theirs not to reason why, Theirs but to do and die."[2] In
this case it was to do *or die*. The right man was on hand
to carry out the order. Marqués de Croix appointed his

1. Clinch, *New Spain,* Vol. I, p. 182.
2. Alfred Lord Tennyson, *Charge of the Light Brigade*—Stanza II.

good friend, the forceful man of action, Don José de Gálvez, who had recently come to New Spain as visitor general of the king.

The next morning, every Jesuit institution, in and within marching distance of Mexico City, was surrounded by a military guard. The officer in charge presented and read the royal order. As passive instruments of royalty, the soldiers performed their duties in the best military manner, yet without abandoning human understanding. At one monastery, the priests were saying their morning Masses when the order was read. The superior asked permission for them to finish. This was granted. Then without protest, each packed his knapsack, taking only essential personal belongings, and left.

Execution of the order took longer in more remote areas. Baja (Lower) California, the narrow, far western peninsula, accessible only by crossing the Gulf of California, had no governor. Don Gaspar de Portolá, appointed by the king, took office for the explicit purpose of expelling the Jesuits.

Despite heavy handed methods, Gálvez was aware that Spain's need for missionaries was extremely critical in the remote areas of the Empire. Gálvez was not a man to move with caution. Seemingly impressed with the importance of his position and certainly eager to proceed with the task before him, he ordered San Fernando College to fill the vacancies in Baja with Franciscans.

The guardian of San Fernando would have appreciated the fine courtesies of consultation and discussion. Gálvez' order pressed an already tight predicament. But in the course of a few months fourteen Franciscans were assembled at San Blas for duty in Baja.

Fr. Serra, who at the time was preaching a mission at Mesquital, some distance from Mexico City, had no previous knowledge of the enterprise until San Fernando ordered him to go to Baja as president. That he had been ordered to this new post gave the zealous missionary joyous assurance that the call had been the will of God and not the consequence of his own solicitation.

On the 14th of March, 1768, after a frustrating period of substitutions, transfers and strenuous traveling, the fourteen Franciscan missionaries, including Serra's special friends and fellow Majorcans, Frs. Palóu, Crespí and Raphael Verger, boarded the *Concepción* and sailed for Loreto. Blown off course by erratic winds, tossed and buffeted, the little ship reached the other side of the narrow channel after two weeks. On Holy Saturday morning, April 2, the missionaries walked in procession from the beach landing to the church, singing "Salve Regina"—a traditional hymn, with a crisp, marching tempo: "Hail, holy Queen, enthroned above, O María! Hail Mother of mercy and of love, O María! Triumph, all ye cherubim, sing with us ye seraphim, heav'n and earth resound the hymn, salve, salve, salve Regina!"

The group celebrated Easter Sunday together at Loreto. After each of the others said a low Mass, Fr. Serra sang a solemn high Mass and preached a moving sermon. Then Portolá, the governor, read the viceroy's letter, legally turning over the missions of the Jesuits to the Franciscans. But contrary to all established missionary procedure and practice, theirs would be spiritual administration of the missions only. All material goods, buildings, furnishings, money and supplies remained the property of the government.

Serra was keenly aware of the problems inherent in such an arrangement. Progress had been particularly slow in these missions. Not too anxious to work or change old ways, the Indians generally were more concerned with a handout of corn, a blanket or trinket than the cultivation of a field or the abstract idea of an infinite God. Some had acquired new skills, while others had not. Government usurpation of mission property could mean the end of the mission movement in Baja California.

Serra had little choice but to acknowledge the letter and promise to conform. His position then, as in future dealings with government officials, was to "Render to Caesar the things that are Caesar's, and to God the things that are God's" (Mt. 22:15-21). He would negotiate when possible, but never give in on matters of principle or those which directly affected the spiritual welfare of his subjects. This was a new assignment. He would take no immediate action but wait for the opportunity to discuss the matter with Gálvez, whom he was confident aspired to progressive support of the missions. He issued assignments to twelve of the fathers, and they left for their respective posts. Fr. Parrón remained at Loreto with Serra.

Great historical movements echo the aspirations, vision and daring of their leaders—men whose character and fortitude are essential to the fulfillment of dreams. Acknowledged apostle of the California missionary movement was the indomitable and beloved Fr. Junípero Serra, man of the cloth, spiritual leader, representative of the Church, ready and eagerly awaiting doors to open. In this joint effort of Church and State, at exactly the right moment, a man appeared whose audacity opened those doors and whose resolution set the whole project afire. Man of the world, representative of the Spanish court, entitled, royally empowered, and newly appointed visitor general of New Spain, was the dynamic, intrepid, ambitious Don Gaspar de Gálvez.

King Carlos had sent Gálvez to New Spain in 1765, with specific instructions to investigate Russian encroachment in California and the possibility of establishing three missions there—one at San Diego, one at Monterey and another halfway between.

Gálvez talked to Marqués de Croix, viceroy of New Spain, and the two leaders agreed it was extremely important to implement the California project with all possible force and haste.

Convening the wisest and ablest talent in Mexico— ship captains, engineers and masons—to discuss the most efficient methods of procedure, Gálvez gave orders to build a naval base at San Blas. A humid, shallow harbor, it was strategically located on the west coast of Mexico. Other orders included building two ships and commanding a third. Three ships should be immediately manned, supplied and conditioned for the hazardous voyage up the coast to San Diego and Monterey. Two land parties would proceed to the north through Baja and meet the ships at San Diego. Portolá would lead the land expeditions, and Serra was named president of the missionary project.

Once everything had been set in motion, Gálvez boarded the *Sinoloa* for Baja. Master of men and affairs on land, the visitor general found himself helpless before the calm of the gulf. With no favorable wind in her sails, the little ship was forty days in crossing the one-hundred mile wide channel.

Finally, ashore in the southern part of the Baja peninsula at Ensenada de Cerralvo, Gálvez lost no time. He wrote Serra of his plans and set up headquarters at

Santa Ana, asking Serra to meet him there to discuss details.

At long last the doors had opened! All that Serra had longed for, hoped for, prayed for was now a reality. He gave orders for the mission bells to ring out, proclaiming the joyous news. Then he celebrated a Mass of thanksgiving. While the bells of Loreto were still ringing, Serra shared his exaltation with the other Baja missionaries by letter, telling them of Gálvez' announcement and suggesting that they, too, ring the mission bells and offer Masses of thanksgiving.

Serra also wrote to Gálvez, congratulating him in the name of all the other Franciscans and stating that he would gladly volunteer his own services "to erect the holy standard of the cross in Monterey,"...to meet the native, to "baptize him in the name of Jesus Christ,"[3] and to found missions in the new land. It seemed more than he had dreamed of. Opportunity had come at last, to carry the cross of Christ to a new land.

In the meantime, Gálvez had been inspecting the missions in the vicinity of Santa Ana. What he saw there and later at the other missions astounded and infuriated him. After a few short months of military occupation, the Baja missions, once thriving and prosperous under the Jesuits, were practically destitute.

In order to tighten the grip on the military and salvage what was left, Gálvez turned all temporalities over to the missionaries, except at Loreto. It was a sort of dichotomous arrangement, however. The missionaries had more leeway of distribution. They could apportion seed and food to the natives, but each was ordered to make an inventory of all goods on hand with perspective and emphasis on systematic and efficient

---

3. Geiger, *op. cit.*, Vol. I, p. 201.

decisions regarding supplies that could be spared for
the Alta California missions.

The Jesuits had dammed the streams, built aqueducts and engineered intricate irrigation systems for
that dry land. They had found no defense against the
devastating hordes of locusts, however, and harvests
had been uncertain. Often food had had to be transported from one mission to another. Still, the Indians
had been living well, and in good seasons they had
produced wheat, corn, beans, rice, oranges, bananas
and cotton and had stored reserve supplies in warehouses for seed and as insurance against crop failure.
Through the years they had built up fine herds of
cattle, which had roamed and thrived on the mission
lands.

Now, with the Jesuits gone and the government in
control, the soldiers had come. They had slaughtered
hundreds of livestock, confiscated warehouse reserves
and damaged mission property, tearing down buildings
for their materials and taking possession of whatever
was handy.

If Gálvez had anticipated reimbursement from the
Baja mission property for the large-scale spending he
had set in motion, this prospect soon faded. But there
was the Pius Fund. In the absence of government support for missionary endeavors, the Jesuits had turned to
their friends, some of whom were wealthy Spaniards,
for donations. These sums of money the fathers had
wisely placed in a capital reserve account, using only
the interest for missionary purposes. Gálvez dipped
deeply into this reserve, his justification being that the
original purpose of the fund was specifically the advancement of Christianity among the natives.

Undismayed, though angry over his discoveries of
military wantonness, Gálvez assigned some of the of-

fending soldiers' overseers to active duty in Sonora. Others were signed for service in Alta California. Then he turned to the Franciscans for restoration of order. Though many essential items had been lost, he did find a surplus of church goods. These he ordered packed for shipment to the Alta California missions.

Serra's old leg infection had persisted through the years, and now, at the critical moment when maximum physical endurance and energy were demanded, it flared into an intensely painful ulcerous condition. But this did not prevent his traveling to the nearby missions. He examined church goods, choosing articles that could be spared for the Alta project. The missionaries made arrangements for packing vestments, chalices, candles, ornaments, statues, linens and bells, as well as agricultural tools, seeds, plants and grain. No less important were brightly colored cloths, beads and trinkets to be given as presents to the Indians of the new land. In all these endeavors the Baja Indians worked with the padres, packing, lugging and transporting the goods from the various missions to La Paz, where they were loaded on the ships.

Barely able to walk, Serra could not conceal his condition from Gálvez who, fearing that the padre would delay the expedition, insisted that he give up the long, arduous land journey. But pain and attempts to discourage him only whetted Serra's determination to go.

The three missions to be founded were already officially named: San Diego de Alcalá, San Carlos at Monterey and San Buenaventura, at an undetermined point. "Is there to be no mission in honor of our holy father, St. Francis?" Serra asked Gálvez. "Let him find the port bearing his name and he will have his mission there,"[4] the visitor general is said to have replied.

New energy and new urgency swept the Baja peninsula. Never before had it known the excitement and noise of so much activity. The fever of adventure was in the air. It reached down through the ranks to everyone, reflecting the spirit of the discovery age, electrifying the thrill of opening new territory—that land of fantastic beauty and enchantment, California.

After bucking capricious gulf winds, the *San Carlos* and *San Antonio,* leaking and listing, limped into La Paz, on the southeast coast of Baja. Both ships were unloaded, careened and repaired. Indians, carpenters, masons, engineers and sailors were all working at high speed. So was Gálvez. Besides organizing and checking accumulating supplies and supervising the work of packing and stowing the cargo, he worked beside the others, caulking, examining the seams, the masts and the entire structure of the ships. And he urged everyone on, anticipating winter storms.

Besides fitting and loading the ships for the first expedition, they built warehouses for the accumulation of supplies to maintain the new settlements. La Paz rang with the sharp, repetitious beat of thudding hammers and bumping lumber, while Indians methodically molded adobe blocks and mixed and carried mortar.

Since September, Don Fernando Rivera y Moncada, former captain in charge of the military unit guarding Loreto, under orders from Gálvez, had been traveling northward from mission to mission gathering cattle and supplies for the Alta California project. Reluctant to criticize, Serra remarked that Rivera's orders to gather supplies had not implied a "raid" on the Baja missions.

---

4. *Ibid.,* Vol. I, p. 204.

Bells echoed their song through history, moving westward with Christian civilization. This tower might have been found in Palma. Actually, it is part of the old Mission San Carlos de Borromeo at Carmel, California.

Church of Santiago at Jalpan, the only remaining structure built by Father Serra. Intricate detail and design indicate unusual architectural and artistic skill.

Mission San Diego de Alcala, Serra's first foundation, though threatened by fire, earthquake and other disasters, has endured. This lovely old structure built in 1808 is located inland from the original site.

1672. Father Serra. The founder of the missions in California is seen with a young Indian convert in the gardens of the Mission San Juan Capistrano, California.

Romantic painting by L. Trousset in 1877 catches the spirit of the dedication of the second mission in Alta California at Monterey a century earlier. A major objective of the expedition from Baja California, the event's significance was reflected in the pageantry observed. When news of the founding reached Mexico City, all the church bells in the city rang out the tidings.

Betty Berg Favello

San Carlos, Carmel, California. The grace of old Spain is wrought by native hands.

Betty Berg Favello

Wooden spanish gate of Mission San Carlos, Carmel, California.

Mission San Carlos Borromeo de Carmelo, founded and built by Father Serra in 1770 and his headquarters until his death in 1784.

Betty Berg Favello

Footsteps through the ages. Old stone steps of Mission San Carlos at Carmel, California.

Mission San Antonio de Padua. Recent restoration has recovered the beauty and charm of this early Spanish-California mission in a valley of California. Founded in 1771, it is again under the direction of the founding Franciscans.

Josef Muench

Mission San Gabriel, fourth of Serra's missions, was founded in 1771. Controlling half a million acres from the mountains to the sea, it was for some twenty years one of the most prosperous of the chain. This present structure was built in 1806 and is now used as a parish church.

Though some have been restored several times, all of Father Serra's missions still stand. San Luis Obisbo, now laced by pepper trees, shows little of the hardships of its early beginnings.

Reflected in the fountain are several of the old mission bells at the Mission San Juan Capistrano. Still in use they peal, with their lovely old voices, ringing out today's hours and reminding us of yesterday's.

Betty Berg Favello

Mission Dolores in San Francisco. The old mission stands at the left and a newer church, bearing the same name stands at the right. Worn stone floors of the interior of the old mission bear the marks of many years of bare-footed worshippers.

Betty Berg Favello

Entrance to the new Mission Dolores, San Francisco, noted for its beautiful Spanish Baroque style.

Betty Berg Favello

Altar at the Mission San Carlos. Father Junipero Serra, Father Juan Crespi and Father Francisco de Lasuen are buried here.

Rivera evidently showed little compassion for the survival of the Baja missions in his eagerness to please Gálvez. He swept the peninsula missions clean, taking livestock, hay, wheat, corn, horses, mules, Indians and soldiers. In each case, he left a receipt for what he took, but the Baja padres complained that this recompense did not satisfy hunger nor help to transfer workers.

Vincent Vila was named captain of the flagship *San Carlos* and commander of the sea expeditions. Finally, in January, 1769, the *San Carlos* was ready to sail. Packed and seaworthy, she quartered sixty-two men. Fr. Hernando Parrón, Serra's assistant at Loreto, was named chaplain. Others included Lieutenant Pedro Fages and his twenty-five Catalán leather-jacketed soldiers; Don Miguel Costansó, an experienced engineer and cosmographer; Dr. Pedro Prat; two blacksmiths; a baker and members of the crew.

Serra's leg was still painful, but it did not prevent his personally going to La Paz for the launching of this great adventure. All members prepared themselves for the expedition by going to confession and receiving the Holy Eucharist. Fr. Serra sang the high Mass, then the visitor general turned orator. He reminded them that each member was an important individual unit in the occupation and security of California in the name of God, the king and the viceroy, and that their names would be written in history. Indeed, the historical outcome of the venture would largely depend on their conduct. They must keep peace among themselves and among the natives. They must always show respect and reverence for the chaplain and the other missionaries. Fr. Serra blessed the assemblage, the flags and the ship. Fr. Parrón knelt for his personal blessing. The little bark then took to the sea. Fr. Serra returned to Loreto and the California operation was on its way.

About a month later, on February 15, the *San Antonio* set sail for Cape San Lucas at the southern tip of the peninsula. Her captain was Don Juan Pérez, a native Majorcan from Palma and seasoned master mariner, who had spent many years in the Pacific piloting Manila galleons between the Philippines and Acapulco. Frs. Vizcaíno and Gómez were the chaplains. The launching ceremony was much the same as for the *San Carlos,* but without Fr. Serra, who was in Loreto, making his own preparations for leaving.

Portolá, as efficient an administrator as he was an able military leader and governor, was busily supervising, organizing, equipping and planning the thousand details that would move an expedition smoothly through rough, unknown territory. His group left Loreto on March 9, and after loading the selected supplies at the various missions, would meet Rivera at Santa María, an agreed meeting place and official starting point for the land expeditions from Baja.

Serra spent Holy Week at Loreto. Mule pack trains moved deliberately and he would have no trouble reaching Santa María at the appointed time. On Easter Tuesday, (anniversary of the Easter Tuesday he had left Petra twenty years before), Serra set out on a broken-down mule, with one Indian boy helper, a loaf of bread and a piece of cheese. A bit of irony slips into his diary as he sums up his year at Loreto: "All the year I passed there I was only a guest of the royal commissary, whose liberality at my parting only extended to the aforesaid bread and cheese."[5] This does not reflect on Portolá, whom Serra liked and admired, but indicates the harassing limitations imposed on the Franciscans by the government usurpation of property. He had had no home to call his own. "A guest," in the governor's

---

5. Tibesar, Vol. I, p. 43.

house, he had been accepted more as a servant. On his arrival, he had been assigned a bed, and also a chair in the dining room. It had been a definite limitation of freedom for one in his official position. Evidently, upon leaving, the aging padre received the same lack of compassion and concern for his comfort.

But others were more thoughtful. He first stopped at Mission San Xavier to see his good friend Palóu, who would remain as president of the Baja missions. Revived by the surging hope of fulfilling a lifelong dream, Serra was still visibly moved by the sadness of parting. Palóu shared his friend's joyous aspirations, but he was justifiably worried about the ulcerous leg. Obviously in serious condition, it was robbing the padre of his natural physical vigor. Confidentially Palóu urged Serra to forego this arduous trip, certain to present untold hazards and hardships that would test the fortitude of the strongest and youngest of men. But his admonitions received the expected firm and simple reply. Serra had placed all his confidence in God and hoped, "He will grant me [the grace] to reach not only San Diego to raise the standard of the holy cross in that port, but also at Monterey."[6] Serra's determination was more impregnable at San Xavier than at Cádiz, when he had written his parents that he would, "Always go forward and never turn back."[7]

When after three days it was time to leave, the infection had so weakened the missionary that he was unable to mount the mule without the help of two strong men, who literally lifted him and adjusted him into the saddle. It was time for farewells. Hoping to call Palóu to California later, Serra said, "Good-bye, Francisco, until we meet in Monterey, where I hope we shall

---

6. *Ibid.*, p. 66.
7. *Ibid.*

see each other and labor in that vineyard of the Lord."[8]
Francisco's less optimistic farewell was, "Good-bye,
Junípero, until eternity."[9]

On his way north, Serra stopped at the various
missions to personally select and arrange for church
supplies to be shipped to the Alta missions. In each
case, the resident priest shared his meager store of
flour, corn, figs and raisins with his beloved superior.
At Guadalupe, Fr. Sancho had spotted a bright Indian
boy of about fifteen, who could speak Spanish, serve
Mass, cook and be generally useful. When he asked his
parents for permission to let him go, they proudly
agreed to this distinctive privilege for their son. The
boy, not only excited about the venture, was elated to
be the master of his own mule and to wear a leather
jacket and accouterment duplicating those worn by the
soldiers. By now, Serra's supplies had so multiplied
from the original loaf of bread and piece of cheese that
he required the help of two lively Indian boys to load
and care for the pack animals.

At Santa Gertrudis, Fr. Donisio Basterra had little
to give. Rivera's "heavy hand" had mercilessly and
pitifully stripped this poor mission, leaving the padre
disconsolate and lonely, with no interpreter, no military
guard, no assistant, a bare minimum of livestock and a
pitifully small group of Indians, mostly old men,
women and children. Serra regretfully could offer Basterra only words of consolation and hopeful promises.

A launch from La Paz, carrying extra supplies for
the expedition, was anchored offshore at Santa María.
Portolá's men were busy unloading this cargo and packing it for the mule train when Serra caught up with the
expedition. Rivera's group had moved ahead, with the

---

8. *Ibid.*
9. *Ibid.*

cattle, to Velicatá's more verdant pasture land. Anxious to get on with the project of the new mission at Velicatá, Serra proposed to Portolá that they move ahead. As it would take at least another four days for the men to finish the packing. Portolá, Serra and Fr. de Campa moved on ahead of the expedition. They could easily cover in one day the distance the mule train would make in two and meet Rivera's group in Velicatá.

On Pentecost Sunday, they cleaned out a little hut to serve as chapel and prepared an altar. In his diary Serra tells us, the soldiers "put on their full accouterment, leather jackets and shields, and with all the surroundings of holy poverty, I celebrated Mass...consoled with the thought that it was the first of many to be continued in this new mission."[10] He blessed the cross they had erected nearby, then officially placed Fr. de Campa in charge of the new mission. But no Indians appeared at the founding of Serra's first mission.

All around were footprints indicating that a large group of Indians lived in the vicinity, but all had run off and hid. Not until the second day after the founding did they appear. When Serra came out of the improvised chapel after saying Mass and giving his thanksgiving, "thanking His Majesty for the fact that, after so many years of looking forward to it, he now permitted me to be among the pagans in their own country,"[11] twelve Indian men and boys stood before him "as naked as Adam in the garden before sin."[12] He filled their hands with figs and Portolá gave them raisins, tobacco leaf and food. The strangers accepted their gifts with friendly appreciation. Then Serra told them, "that the Father would be their best friend and these gentlemen,

---

10. *Ibid.*, p. 71.
11. *Ibid.*, p. 72.
12. *Ibid.*, p. 63.

the soldiers who are to stay with the Father, would do them much good and no harm; that they must not steal the cattle; when in need call the Father."[13]

One day out of Velicatá, Serra's leg infection caused so much pain that he could neither walk nor stand, threatening to fulfill all those dire predictions that he would become a stretcher case. Portolá, on whose shoulders rested all responsibility for leading the expedition to San Diego, was sympathetic but practical. He suggested that since they were still in familiar territory Serra could easily turn back now. Serra replied again, as at San Xavier, "I shall not turn back."[14] They could bury him among the natives, but he would not turn back.

Fortunately for Serra, the expedition had stopped to rest. Ortega, the scout, had discovered that San Juan de Dios was, as Serra described it, "an agreeable spot, with abundant water, pasture, willows, tules and a smiling sky,"[15] a fine place for the livestock to renew their strength before the long push ahead into rough, unknown lands. For the first time, all members of the two land expeditions were together. Serra found joy in the reunion, but his leg showed no sign of healing.

He prayed for relief, that he would not hold the rest back, then asked one of the muleteers, "Son, do you know how to prepare a remedy for the wound in my foot and leg?"

The muleteer, surprised at his sudden promotion to medical practitioner, replied, "Why, Father,...I am a muleteer; I've healed only the sores of animals."

---

13. *Ibid.*

14. *Ibid.*

15. *Ibid.*

"Well then, son," said Serra, "just imagine that I am an animal." [16]

The muleteer prepared a poultice of herbs, and the next day Serra was so much improved that he said Mass and was able to proceed with the group.

The willow shade of San Juan faded into memory as the long, plodding line of mules, horses, cattle and men kicked up clouds of dry, loose, hot sand; the sun beat down with pitiless intensity. But encouraging news brought by courier from Fr. de Campa brightened the day for Serra. Forty-four Indians had come to the new mission at Velicatá and asked for Baptism. Now he knew that his first mission would be a success.

Day after tiring day, they plodded the hazardous miles of dust and desolation under a scorching desert sun. It was a land of solitude and harshness, of waterless desert and steep, rocky ravines. "Sometimes with the greatest difficulty [we were] climbing up and down hills, without any intermission." They struggled through prickly cactus jungles, ancient palm-tree-filled canyons, dry lake beds and fertile green valleys. Then the terrain changed to great masses of barren white rocks, broken and jagged, which blocked their passage and forced them to detour.

The northern section of Baja was more fertile, covered with tall grass, large oak trees, wild grapes and colorful flowers. Serra noted locations suitable for future missions and became ecstatic over the wild roses, "the queen of flowers, the rose of Castile...blessed be he who created them." [17]

But all was not roses. Death had preceded them. "Here we came across the grave of one of the Indians who went on ahead with the captain [Rivera]. His

---

16. *Ibid.*
17. *Ibid.*, p. 105.

bones were scattered. We collected them and buried them again. Either the natives or the wild animals had dug out the grave."[18]

Indians of different temperaments appeared along the way. At times some followed peaceably on the crests of nearby hills, then disappeared. One group, actually hostile, confronted the Spaniards with bows and arrows, demanding that they turn back. As a warning, mounted soldiers shot twice into the air. At this, the Indians fled. Another group "of a more pleasing character...very politely" gave them mescal and "laid all their weapons on the ground," then acted out a sort of pantomime war, taking the part of both the attacked and the attacker, giving the Spaniards a good laugh.[19]

At one point "one of the mule drivers discovered a silver mine, which all declare to be very rich," Serra muses, and wishes, "May it bring them a fortune."[20] At last, "from a hilltop we saw the West Coast Sea that we had been so anxious to reach. We identified this place with what is called on the maps and sea charts: La Ensenada de Todos Santos."[21] This "small bay of all the saints" is no doubt the inlet along the northern coast of Baja where the now popular resort town of Ensenada is located.

The last, long, difficult miles seemed endless, but the little party of intrepid Iberian pioneers finally reached their primary goal. On the morning of July 1, from a rise they glimpsed the tip of San Diego Bay. Still they must travel five more tedious hours before, from another hilltop, they could see the entire bay and the two ships, the *San Carlos* and *San Antonio*, at anchor

18. *Ibid.*, p. 85.
19. *Ibid.*, p. 77.
20. *Ibid.*, p. 97.
21. *Ibid.*, p. 105.

there. The California project had successfully attained
its initial objective and western Christendom had
stretched a new frontier. Now, all four expeditions
were united. Serra wrote, "It was a day of much rejoic-
ing and merriment for all...and [we] gave great thanks
to God, who after all, had brought us together there."[22]
His dreams and prayers of forty years had been answered.

A new horizon of the Spanish domain had opened,
that Christendom might grow and "become the Great
Society, a tree in whose branches all nations of the
earth might come and lodge."[23]

---

22. *Ibid.*
23. Arnold J. Toynbee, *A Study of History,* p. 125.

Harbor
for St. Francis

Serra looked down on the sparkling, blue San Diego Bay. Now an impressive reality of the centuries-old mystical dream, he proclaimed it "truly beautiful to behold" and worthy of the fame attributed to it by Cabrillo in 1542, and again sixty years later by Vizcaíno. Snugly locked between two protective land points, the bay lay peaceful and calm, waiting still and silent as it had through the long years. And bobbing on the clear, smooth surface, the *San Carlos* and *San Antonio* rode at anchor waiting. Rivera's small land party and the cattle had arrived six weeks earlier. But congratulations and friendly reunions were at once mingled with sorrow.

The *San Antonio* had successfully made the trip in fifty-five days, but the *San Carlos,* blown off course south to Panama, had been 110 days enroute. And leaky water barrels had forced the crew to stop and take on fresh water, which the voyagers claimed was impure. Whether due to contaminated water or other causes, the crew had developed scurvy, and the *San Carlos* dropped anchor at San Diego practically a ghost ship. Without hesitation, the *San Antonio's* able-bodied men went to the aid of their disabled companions, and they too became infected. Everyone praised Dr. Prat for his untiring perseverance and solicitude, but neither kindness nor skill could save the men from this agonizing plague of the sea. When the Portolá-Serra expedition arrived, all but five of the *San Carlos* crew were dead and only seven of the *San Antonio* crew had survived.

Serra and the other priests worked relentlessly night and day, caring for and comforting the sick, giving them the last anointing, saying funeral Masses and burying the dead.

Portolá, in conference with Captain Rivera and the other officers, reassessed the situation and agreed that the wisest plan was for the *San Antonio*, manned with the surviving sailors, to sail immediately for San Blas and recruit a double crew of men and supplies. Portolá and his men, still hale and hearty, could carry on in the fulfillment of the objectives of the expedition and Gálvez' orders, by setting out promptly for Monterey.

Accordingly, the *San Antonio* left San Diego on July 9. Several members of the meager crew succumbed to the disease on the voyage, but Juan Pérez, the indomitable master mariner of the Pacific, once more proved his seafaring proficiency and grim determination, and the *San Antonio* arrived safely at San Blas twenty days later.

Five days after the *San Antonio's* departure from San Diego, Portolá, with seventy-four men—including Captain Rivera; Lieutenant Fages; Costansó, the engineer; Sergeant Ortega; Frs. Crespí and Gómez; muleteers; a group of Baja Indians and a contingent of

Catalán leather-jacketed soldiers—started north in search of the fabled harbor of Monterey.

While this troop of valiant Iberian explorers laboriously progressed through California hills and valleys and along the rugged sea coasts, a pitifully small and weakened group waiting at San Diego faced troublesome times. This group consisted of Captain Vila of the *San Carlos;* Corporal Juan Puig; a blacksmith; a carpenter; Dr. Prat; Frs. Serra, Parrón and Vizcaíno; Serra's two Indian boys; eight Baja Indians; a few sailors, who had not been well enough to sail on the *San Antonio* and eight soldiers, all suffering scurvy. They totaled forty persons, more than half of whom were incapacitated.

Despite this holocaust of human misery, preliminary steps were taken for founding the mission. Essential to the success of every mission were an abundance of water, productive soil and a substantially large group of natives. Even before Portolá left, Serra and Crespí had investigated the San Diego River, flowing through the rolling hills down into the bay, and concluded that though it was a shallow stream in summer, it appeared to be a continuous and reliable source of water. The missionaries, trained in the skills of irrigation engineering, would be able to construct the necessary dams, aqueducts and drainage systems to fulfill human needs and raise crops.

Scouting the land, they found it "plentiful and good."[1] They could envisage the rolling hills pasturing growing herds of cattle; grain in the deeper soil of the valleys, ripening and flowing in the breeze; vegetables maturing and fruit trees blossoming in the spring, hopeful of summer harvest. Large sycamore, oak, willow and poplar trees testified to the special fertility of isolated silt deposits, where luxuriated "Castile" roses

---

1. Serra's letter to Fray Andrés, 7-3-1769, Tibesar, p. 137.

bloomed, grapevines climbed with abandon into spreading trees and wild asparagus sprouted fern-like along the banks of streams. Acorns supplied an affluent diet for the natives as well as deer and antelope. Bear, wolves, coyotes and innumerable small animals roamed the hills, and the air was full of the song of birds.

Though the land appeared promising, it was apparent that the Indians would present a problem. They had an exasperating habit of stealing and stole everything that had been left unguarded, convincing some of the Spaniards that the devil was in them.

But Serra saw them only as souls to be saved. He wrote to Fr. Andrés, guardian of San Fernando, "Already God, our Lord, has placed into the hands of the holy college [San Fernando] this most abundant harvest.... May God give them and us his holy grace, so that in a short time all will become Christians." [2] Only a heart consumed with the fire of faith and impelled by a consuming love could project the Indians' conversion as children of God. To this persistence of dynamic purpose, western civilization owes its strength.

Despite all obstacles, two days after the bustle and confusion of Portolá's departure, on the morning of July 16, Serra founded Mission San Diego de Alcalá, the first of the Alta California missions and actually the first of Serra's own. Velicatá would fall to the jurisdiction of others, but San Diego was and would be Serra's responsibility—the realization of a spiritual dream—a new mission in new lands, among pagans who seemingly had had no previous contact with anything relating to Christianity, and whose appearance would tend to belie any hope of future acceptance of God or of a civilizing influence.

---

2. *Ibid.*

On top of the hill, now known as Presidio Hill, overlooking the bay, the able-bodied men set up a few small grass huts for shelter. The largest of these, in which they erected an altar, qualified as a temporary church. Here, on that July morning, commemorating Our Lady of Mount Carmel, Fr. Serra said the Mass. Then he blessed and dedicated the large wooden cross erected in front of the church, signifying the purpose and location of a mission. With the Cross of Christ now officially blessed and planted on California soil, Serra ardently prayed for the salvation of those pagan souls whom he hoped the grace of God would eventually enlighten.

But the Indians he longed to reach had witnessed neither the proceedings nor the spirit of the ceremony. They hid out. One cause of trouble from the first was the language barrier. Serra had gone to great lengths to bring Baja Indians as interpreters, hoping they might find basic language similarities with the Alta California Indians. But the San Diego dialect bore no similarity to any Baja dialect, nor to any other known dialect of New Spain.

We now know that in California alone, the Indians spoke over one hundred separate dialects, among which there was little or no mutual understanding. These dialects formed eighteen major languages, which in turn fitted into six separate language families, having no common relationship or origin. At first, both Indian and Spaniard were limited to sign communication.

The friendship of one young boy offered a slim hope of spanning this gap. From the least hostile of the different villages or groups into which the natives were divided, came a boy about the age of Serra's Baja page boys, who showed not only every indication of wanting to be friendly, but also a lively interest in learning

Spanish words. Through this association began a code
of intercommunication.

Despite this fragile link, the Indians daily became
more unfriendly and malicious. They came regularly to
the mission and the camps and accepted gifts, but
always with snarling insistence that they be given more
or something else that appealed to them. They would
wander into the infirmary, ridicule the patients, pull
the sheets and blankets off the beds, and at the first
unguarded moment, run off with them. In desperation,
the soldiers would shoot into the air to frighten them
off. Unimpressed, they would mimic the soldiers, dancing around crazily and yelling, "Bang! Bang!"

All in all, the first months at San Diego were long,
agonizing and frustrating. Until the mood of the natives
changed, missionary activity stood still. As the missionaries waited anxiously for news from Portolá and for
the arrival of another ship, the misery, suffering and
horror of scurvy—its rotted gums; lost teeth; swollen,
scarred, useless limbs and slow, painful, helpless
death—continued day and night. Both Fr. Serra and
Fr. Vizcaíno became infected with the plague, but recovered with no serious consequences. It was a time of
constant trial, but Serra heroically endured all hardships, accepting them as the sacrificial foundation of
the missionary endeavor; the cross before the resurrection.

And matters grew worse. On August 15, with
sneaky cunning, the Indians chose a propitious moment, a moment of changing the guard, when only a
minimum number of Spaniards were at the camp.
While the men were on their way between the camp
and the ship, twenty natives, armed with bows and
arrows, attacked the mission.

A miniature battle ensued. Four armed Spaniards fought the Indians off, but the arrows found their mark. Three Spaniards, including Fr. Vizcaíno, were wounded. The tragedy of the day, however, was the loss of Serra's beloved and faithful Baja Indian boy, the one who had come all the way with him from Loreto. An arrow pierced his neck and he ran bleeding to Serra, "Father, absolve me; the Indians have killed me."[3] He died at Serra's feet in a pool of blood, but with the blessing and absolution of the apostle of California.

Three natives were killed and several others wounded. They had learned the painful and mortal bite of Spanish guns and grew more respectful. Dr. Prat cared for the Indians, as he did for the Spaniards, dressing their wounds and nursing them back to health. His gentleness contributed to a more agreeable attitude, at least for a time.

Serra had always resisted any kind of wall or barrier separating the mission from the natives. After this brawl, however, he submitted to the soldiers' insistence on building a stockade around the buildings and keeping the Indians out.

Months wore on. Undisturbed by the hostilities, the young San Diego Indian boy continued to visit the Spanish camp and to ask questions. His growing knowledge of Spanish words and reciprocal exchange of native expressions opened wider avenues of understanding and friendship. Soon he was carrying messages to his people, explaining the Spaniards' purpose and their peaceful intentions. From this contact, Serra not only built a basic vocabulary, but was able to establish perceptive communication and to relate to his would-be converts.

---

3. Geiger, *Palóu's Life of Fray Junípero,* p. 77.

The old year slipped into the new and about noon on January 24, 1770, someone spotted Portolá's men coming home. Haggard, dirty, half starved, and smelling of mule, all seventy-four hardened explorers struggled into camp, grateful to be back alive, but with strange news. There was no Monterey Bay! They had discovered a magnificent bay, farther north, a harbor large enough to hold the ships of Europe. But nothing they had seen fitted the explorer Vizcaíno's "O" shaped, sheltered bay of Monterey.

Time was running out. Practically devoid of food, supplies and patience, Serra and his companions could offer the travelers little sustenance. Once more the joy of reunion was marred by gnawing pangs of anguish. San Diego's supplies, stretched further by the arrival of Portolá's seventy-four hungry men, could not last long. Surpassing the ordeal of deprivation were the interminable stench and misery of scurvy, and lingering over all was the ever-present threat and reality of death. During Portolá's absence, nineteen more men had been buried in California soil.

Hope was waning for the help that should have come. The *San José* was long overdue. The *San Antonio* should soon return. In the event that either might have by-passed San Diego, Portolá could testify that they had not appeared in the vicinity of Monterey.

Had the members of the expedition known what they, no doubt, suspected regarding the fate of the *San José,* discouragement could indeed have terminated the enterprise. On her voyage north the *San José* had run into head winds and had been blown back to Acapulco. After repairs had been made, the ship had sailed again—into oblivion. With her, besides her captain and other personnel, went a cargo that included richly embroidered vestments, altar cloths, statues and gold and silver altar vessels. No trace of her was ever found. Sea support of the California expedition had been practically a disaster.

Early in February, Captain Rivera with twenty soldiers, three muleteers and Fr. Vizcaíno, who had not fully recovered from his Indian battle scars, left for Velicatá to bring back cattle and supplies. The experienced and efficient Rivera would spur on with all possible speed, but a cattle drive over the rugged Baja terrain between Velicatá and San Diego would take time. Even the most optimistic calculations could not estimate that the dwindling supplies at San Diego would hold out until his return.

The premises were as clear as a blackboard chart. The conclusion left but one recourse. There was no need of further evidence to prove Portolá's loyalty and devotion to the project, but he was not about to sit there and subject the entire assemblage to slow death by starvation. He told Serra he had decided to return with his men to La Paz.

Serra, also a practical man, could see the logic of Portolá's decision, but he was dedicated to a dream, a spiritual dream that would not die. He knew that once Portolá and his men left San Diego, the California project was doomed. He pleaded with Portolá and prayed to his God. And confirming his stand, he made a pact with Fr. Crespí that, come what might, neither would go back. The two intrepid priests had an ally in Captain Vila of the *San Carlos*, who was equally determined never to abandon his ship.

Persistent, persuasive and confident enough in Divine Providence to make a spiritual gamble, Serra induced Portolá to agree to a plan. Beginning on March 10, Serra would conduct a novena to St. Joseph, patron saint of the expedition. If help did not come by the 19th, Portolá and his men would be free to leave.

The fate of California's missions hung on the outcome of those nine days. Serra began the novena. Everyone participated. But none prayed as fervently as Serra. All his hope, his love, his faith rose beseechingly to heaven, imploring Almighty God, his divine Son, the holy Mother, St. Joseph and all the saints to send help; to save the missions; to allow the light of truth to be brought to the thousands of souls who lived in darkness in this beautiful land. All day he prayed and most of every night. Yet each day was the same.

The sun rose over the green hills and set in the changeless, plangent sea. Each day they watched from Presidio Hill, and searching from horizon to horizon, saw only the blue, flat, endless sea. The morning of the 19th was the same. All received Holy Communion and the novena was over. Still there was no sign of a ship. Then at three o'clock that afternoon, someone called out, "Sail!" All looked out and from Presidio Hill, they could see a white speck rising above the horizon. Like a phantom, off in the distance, it appeared again, then vanished. There was no mistake, no illusion. All knew it was a sail. They could not know if it would return. Now, Portolá could not leave.

It was the *San Antonio.* Under orders to sail to Monterey, she was bound northward when they glimpsed her sails. A short time after they spotted her, she ran into trouble and stopped in the Santa Barbara Channel. The friendly Indians there came out in small boats to greet the Spanish ship. By means of signs they told Pérez that Portolá's expedition had returned to San Diego. Pérez quickly comprehended the situation and gave orders to turn back at full sail. Three days later the *San Antonio* dropped anchor in San Diego Bay and the California project was saved.

With fresh men, abundant supplies and new hope, Portolá promptly made arrangements for the second land expedition to leave for Monterey. Supplies needed for his foray and those required at San Diego were unloaded. Everything else remained stored aboard the *San Antonio,* which would sail for Monterey and a rendezvous with Portolá.

The first expedition had netted for Portolá and the others valuable experience and knowledge. For one thing, they had established the fact that the Indians north of San Diego were friendly and peaceful and that no formidable protective army was needed. On this trip Portolá would take about half the number of men and supplies of the first expedition. This would appreciably lighten their burden and speed progress. Portolá; his servant boy; Lieutenant Fages; Costansó, the indispensable engineer; five Baja Indians and Fr. Crespí, chaplain and diarist, were included in this experienced and seasoned group of explorers.

Sergeant José Francisco Ortega with eight soldiers would remain to protect San Diego along with twelve Baja Indians, Frs. Parrón and Gómez, and the faithful Captain Vila, who would rather die than abandon his crewless ship.

All personnel of both contingents attended Mass at San Diego on Easter Sunday. It was their last reunion. The next morning Captain Pérez weighed anchor and the *San Antonio,* with Fr. Serra aboard, set sail for Monterey. Portolá's expedition left the following day, April 17, 1770.

For the land party, the second trip was a smooth revisitation of familiar territory and amiable people. It was clear that the first expedition had left a most favorable impression, for on their return the natives welcomed them as friends. Fr. Crespí, ever thinking of possible mission sights, had noted on the first expedition, as they traveled along the Los Ángeles River: "This plain where the river runs is very extensive. It has good land for planting all kinds of grain and seeds and is the most suitable site of all that we have seen for a mission, for it has all the requisites for a large settlement."[4]

But the Santa Barbara reports were still more glowing. The Indians there had developed a good civilization. They lived in towns of five hundred to one thousand people, built thatched-roofed houses and carved out skillfully constructed wooden canoes, provided with smoke holes in the center of a cabin, and sturdy enough for deep-water tuna fishing. Signs, now an accepted language, told the Spaniards that enemies from the mountains would periodically stage violent raids, burning and destroying their huts and villages.

Only thirty-eight days after leaving San Diego, on Ascension Day, May 14, 1770, Portolá's party arrived at Monterey, all in good health. The sea was empty of ship or sail. Portolá, Crespí and a small military guard went directly to the site of a cross they had erected near Carmel on the last trip. It stood just as they had left it, except that it was arrayed with gifts. Arrows and feathers had been carefully placed around the base and strings of sardines and dried meat hung from the arms, but no Indians could be seen. Accepting this as a sign of good will, the Spaniards concluded that the Indians were shy, but friendly. Then they pushed on with the task of locating elusive Monterey Bay.

---

4. Crespí's Diary, August 2, 1769, *Palóu's New California*, VII. (Dr. H. E. Bolton, who 150 years later, fully retraced every mile of Fr. Crespí's travels, states that this is the present site of the city of Los Ángeles).

First, they explored from the look-out points on the hills above the sea. Below them, clearly and unmistakably, lay the large "O" shaped bay, sheltered by the Point of Pines on one side and the Point Año Nuevo on the other. It was the picture they had expected to find the last time, matching in detail the words of Bueno: a harbor smooth as a lake, with the Pacific Ocean beyond. Large schools of seals splashed and played in the placid blue water. The subsequent discovery of San Francisco Bay had defined the location of Monterey as south of San Francisco, and consequently they conceded that the "open bay" they had seen was indeed Monterey, but as they reasoned, changed by time.

Portolá's group set up camp at Carmel, which they had found before to be a more suitable campsite, well protected and with a constant supply of fresh water. Through millennia the Indians, too, had selected this as the most favorable area for their home grounds. No sooner had the Spaniards established camp, then the natives appeared with gifts of seeds and venison, their prize possessions. It was clearly indicated that the mutual exchange of gifts and sign communication was leading to a comfortable association.

The days passed slowly. At the end of a week, a sail rose over the horizon. As previously agreed, the landsmen signaled their presence by setting three fires and the *San Antonio* acknowledged with canon salvos. Pérez evidently found Bueno's nautical directions faultless, for without incident, the little packet-boat entered Monterey Bay and dropped anchor. The following day, launches took Crespí, Portolá and others aboard to celebrate the culmination of another successful step in the California project and to make plans for establishing the second California mission.

On Pentecost Sunday, Mission San Carlos de Borromeo was established at Monterey.

In 1602, when Vizcaíno had entered the harbor, he had had aboard three Carmelite fathers, chaplains of the expedition. They had gone ashore and said Mass. Bueno had minutely described the location, under a great oak tree beside Monterey Bay. Portolá's party had no difficulty finding the same tree, down by the beach, near a ravine, "whose branches bathe in the sea at high tide."

Here, on the same spot, 168 years later, Portolá's men set up a small altar. All members of the land and sea expeditions assembled—leather-jacketed soldiers, white-bloused sailors, plume-hatted Portolá and black-haired Baja Indian boys. Bells hanging from the tree rang out across the bay and reverberated through the hills, breaking the silence of nearly two centuries. Strangers heard and wondered, but did not appear.

Serra blessed the large, crude cross, which the men had hewn from timber found nearby. Serra wrote, "We all assisted in raising it and I blessed it, chanting the prayers of benediction. Then we planted it in the ground and all of us venerated it with all the tenderness of our hearts. With holy water I blessed those fields. Thus with the standard of the King of Heaven raised, the standards of our Catholic monarch were also set up, the one ceremony being accompanied by shouts of 'Long live the faith!' and the other by 'Long live the king!' Added to this was the clangor of cannonading from the back."[5]

Then Serra sang the Mass—"All the while there was cannonading"—and they closed the ceremonies by singing "Salve Regina."[6]

---

5. Tibesar, p. 169.
6. *Ibid.*

Serra's second California mission had been established. The religious ceremonies completed, the roughshod, imperious Fages, geared up for action, plunged into the business of building construction with a vengeance. Costansó, the engineer, assisted in selecting sites for the presidio and mission and drew up the plans. Portolá's camp was moved to Monterey, the scene of operations. All agreed that Serra and Crespí would be more comfortable aboard the *San Antonio* until their quarters were available.

The soldiers were put to work. They unloaded the *San Antonio's* cargo, cut lumber, and performed all the tasks of construction.

Her work accomplished, the *San Antonio* sailed out of Monterey harbor on July 9, 1770, exactly one year from the day she had sailed from San Diego on her first rescue mission. With her went Serra's letter to Gálvez, describing the joyous ceremonies on the occasion of the establishment of San Carlos Mission on Pentecost and graciously thanking the visitor general for the beautiful statue of Mary most holy, "which gave this wilderness a look of pious elegance."[7] Upon receipt of this letter, Gálvez asked that all the bells in Mexico City ring in joyous celebration of the good news that at long last the first two California missions had been successfully established and the Spanish frontier secured.

Serra wrote to Fray Andrés, guardian of San Fernando, asking for more priests, but warning that life would not be easy. Once before in San Diego, he had written: "To sum up, those who are to come here as ministers should not imagine that they come for any other purpose than to put up with hardships for the love of God and the salvation of souls.... The distances are great...communication by sea makes it necessary

---

7. *Ibid.*, p. 185.

that they endure.... But to a willing heart all is sweet, 'amanti suave est.'"[8] And again from Monterey, he reminded the guardian general, "Hardships they will have to face—these men who come to sacrifice themselves in so holy an enterprise—as everyone knows."[9]

Besides Serra's letters, aboard the *San Antonio* were Costansó and Portolá. Explorer and discoverer of San Francisco Bay, Portolá will ever be revered by Californians for his ingenious leadership and indomitable courage. Straightforward and unflinching, intelligent and practical, with a full measure of vision and foresight, he could quickly perceive all aspects of a situation and act with discerning wisdom and dispatch. And combined with the superior complexities of leadership were the simplicities of compassion that won the affection and respect of his men and all who worked with him. Especially important to the California project were his kindness and generosity, which won and established the friendship and good will of the natives, a potent psychological victory for the missionary endeavor.

The sails of the *San Antonio* slipped away and disappeared over the horizon. Left in Monterey, this far western boundary of the Spanish Empire, were forty men. Almost a year of anxious waiting lay ahead before they would again receive supplies or have any contact with the civilized world.

---

8. *Ibid.*, p. 139.
9. *Ibid.*, p. 173.

Building, Planning and Frustration

Before boarding the *San Antonio,* Portolá had warned Fages that under all circumstances he, as military commander, must remember that the primary purpose of the Alta California conquest was to extend the faith. The cross must precede the flag. This balanced and sagacious advice, the insensate Fages was lamentably incapable of embracing.

Fages was strictly a military man: a career man. As military commander he now had power—power he had never before thought obtainable. His new titles "Commander in Chief" and "Representative of the King" resounded with status and nobility. But if the lieutenant appraised his new titles with awe, he more realistically evaluated his responsibilities with fear.

Of immediate concern was the constant probability of a major uprising among the thousands of natives surrounding them. He was very much aware that his pitifully small military unit would be totally incapable of handling such a disturbance. Equally frightening was the remote—but, nevertheless, uncomfortably real— threat of foreign invasion. And overriding all else was the ominous certainty that his own personal career hinged on so fragile a situation.

Unfortunately, absorption in this limited outlook precluded a greater vision. Fages could not perceive that his coveted advancement would be determined by the success of the California project, and that both his career and advancement actually rested on the overall administrative policy of friendly cooperation with the Franciscan missionaries.

For all his apprehension, Fages was enterprising, energetic, strong-willed and an autocratic driver. His first task was to provide shelter for the little group newly arrived on foreign shores. He ordered the men to work with as much drive and bravado as they would have had charging into battle. Soldier and sailor turned carpenter and mason, working from sunrise to sunset every day of the week. There was nothing like a dose of solid work to keep their minds occupied, the commander theorized. Everyone worked: the priests, the Indian boys, the muleteers. The ring of axe and thud of hammers echoed and re-echoed through pine forests and rose above the distant, but ever present roar of surf. Buildings took shape, enclosed by a protective, high pine-log stockade.

Fages, Dr. Prat and the military personnel lived in the presidio, or main oblong building. The other building served two purposes. The largest section was used for storing reserve supplies and the rest was divided into a palisade of separate rooms, which due to Fages' idiosyncrasies, proved to be something of a jail. The lieutenant, whom Serra called a "ridiculous little fellow," insisted upon keeping the keys to their cells, so he could "lock us in and out when he pleased."[1]

Serra was amused by these minor personal inconveniences. Still, as he reflected on the mood of the fledgling camp, he saw growing indications of problems and dilemmas. Fages, an ordinary little man, a good first sergeant, had been given authority far above his capacity. He had driven the men too hard. They were complaining to Serra. He pleaded their case, and was practically told to mind his own business. Tempers and resentment rose. The men were on the verge of rebellion. Serra saw the irony of the situation. Once the immediate task was completed, Fages would turn them all loose to loiter and roam at will. Lack of orderly, planned military discipline would disrupt the harmonious climate essential for progress.

Serra's more serious concern, however, was that, with Portolá gone, Fages showed every indication of assuming autocratic control of the missionaries and the missions. This was contrary to the intent of the project and in direct opposition to military orders.

Spanish bureaucracy left ample room for conflict in authority between religious and civil authorities. Regulations clearly specified that the military should not interfere with the work of the missionaries. Conversely, the missionaries had no control of the military. Confusion, frustration and friction were inevitable. Basically, the military were there to conquer. The missionaries were there to teach. Idealistically the government, represented by the military, and the Church, represented by the missionaries, were to be of one mind, pursuing one goal. The only recourse was the voice of authority and mediation, the viceroy in far-off Mexico City.

---

1. Geiger, *Life...*, Vol. I, p. 279.

Serra resolved to avoid confrontation if possible, and looked with pride and gratitude on the actual foundation of a mission in elusive Monterey.

By now he had seen enough of California to know that it was truly a land of compelling wonderment. Vast and free, it lay unrestricted by pomp and panoply, solemn in its silent, propitious promise. The surging, restless sea; the great, towering snow-capped mountains; the land—the rich, fertile land, burgeoning with life-sustaining wealth—waited. How long it had been waiting, no one knew, but soon now, men would come. They would overflow the land, stir the soil, build, teach, grow, multiply. It all made "now" singularly urgent. This brief interim of time had been opened to them. It soon would pass. This was the moment preserved in history for teaching these poor, hidden people before they would become absorbed into a pluralistic society.

Serra's spirit, aspirations, imagination and zeal rose to heights he had never known before. He envisioned missions the full length of California...from Loreto to San Francisco, with a day's travel between each one and the next. Certainly, it was the wishful thinking of a man of vision. Genius, it might be called in the scientific world; sanctity, perhaps, in the spiritual world. Serra's visions, however, were not outside the realm of possibility. But possibility required the cooperation of the military and others involved.

Actually, Serra's "vision" was no illusion. His was the only practical plan that would work. Two feeble missions separated by four hundred miles of wilderness had no hope of survival. They had made progress in California, but the victory was not yet won. Ominously without infused purpose and drive the entire project faced disaster. Only the solidarity of a well connected chain of productive units could make any impression on the thousands of natives. The same cooperative awareness was essential in facing internal strife or foreign invasion. In Serra's Majorcan heritage there was no room for fear—only straight-forward, hard work to get the job done. Face the problem and tackle it day by day.

In a confidential burst of reckless enthusiasm, and relying on the mutual vision of a friendship in which both understood the same language of boundless love, the love of eternity, he had written to Fray Andrés, guardian of San Fernando: he could use a hundred missionaries!

But the complexity of interwoven governmental and Church relationship through which he must work was definitely bound by irretractable limitations of vision, the limitation of goods, the limitation of fear. Serra's dream was subject to the restraining walls of all these.

In the immeasurable time it took letters from California to reach their Mexican destination, Fray Andrés had been replaced by Fray Raphael Verger, Serra's friend, a fellow Majorcan—the very man, in fact, who had burst into Palóu's cell back in Palma with news that one of their own was planning to go to the New World as a missionary. Fr. Verger was a dedicated Franciscan, devout and sympathetic to the missionary ideal. But Verger was strictly and sedately a conservative man of facts, dates and figures. "One hundred men! The man must be out of his mind!" This was Verger's reaction to Serra's letter.

Gálvez, Serra's political counterpart with regard to welfare of the missions, was still in Mexico City. In the two years since he had launched the project, his enthusiasm, vision and zeal had remained constant but his diplomacy had grown even more blunt and crude. He contacted San Fernando. Forty-nine missionaries had just arrived from Spain, new and eager, but green. Gálvez requested Verger to send all forty-nine to Alta California immediately. This was impossible, Verger irritatingly maintained. They needed rest, training and adjustment. The somewhat heated exchange of letters finally led to compromise. Thirty men would be sent to California, twenty for Palóu in Baja and ten for Serra in Alta. The new year, 1771, was but twenty days old when the *San Antonio* sailed again from San Blas for Alta with the ten new missionaries aboard.

In the meantime, back in Monterey, Serra's mounting urge to go forward was halted. Like a prisoner, he waited. That Monterey was not a favorable location for a mission became more apparent each day. But he must wait—wait for permission from the viceroy to move the mission to the logical and more suitable spot, Carmel, three miles away. He must wait for the Indians. Small groups of natives came to the Monterey compound. They were friendly and readily accepted the padre's gifts, but they showed no eagerness to work. The major villages were at Carmel. Under the circumstances, no regular mission routine was possible. It would have to wait.

One bright moment came, however, on December 26, 1770. A native couple brought their five-year-old son to the mission, asking that he be baptized. This, Serra's first Alta California baptism, was a fine Christmas present and a hopeful portent for the new year.

One of the Baja Indian boys, who had been associating with the Carmel natives, soon discovered that he could understand their language. It was a language of sounds and "grunts" without benefit of alphabet, but out of it Serra formed a basic vocabulary—the key that opened the door of understanding. Serra now could translate the liturgy and Christian doctrinal teaching into the native tongue of the Carmel Indians. The dialogue worked both ways. In turn, the natives were using Spanish words and expressions. Serra always opened to them the arms of friendship, accompanied by small gifts and the greeting, "Amar a Dios!" ("Love God!") This soon became the mutually accepted salutation not only between Spaniard and native, but among the Indians themselves. It was a delightful surprise to Spaniards just arriving in the new land to hear from the natives the familiar "Amar a Dios!" or "Vaya con Dios!" ("Go with God!") In the west today, is frequently heard the more abbreviated form, "Adios!"

The long, lonely days passed into weeks, and weeks and months grew into a challenge of patience and endurance as no ship came with news or supplies from the outside world. Vegetables from Serra's and Fages' gardens provided sustenance when staples gave out. Spring had called green shoots from the earth with promise of abundant crops, but these withered and died before harvest. The newcomers had much to learn about growing wheat, corn and beans in Alta California. The flat land near the sea proved to be salty and though flowers bloomed profusely in the area, more sunshine was essential for the crops.

Almost two years after she had sailed away, the white sails of the *San Antonio* rose over the horizon and the little ship dropped anchor once more in the harbor of Monterey.

Ten new missionaries disembarked and Serra was jubilant. The first mail in two years included letters from Gálvez and Verger. Serra had permission to move the San Carlos mission to Carmel, and the doors were opened for new missions.

Fages had mail too. Of first interest to him was his commission as captain. This promotion was in keeping with his position as commander of the military in Alta California. A letter from Gálvez told the commander that there should be no delay now in founding the new missions. Missionaries and supplies were aboard, and Rivera was on his way to San Diego with more men. The long postponed San Buenaventura should be founded immediately and one mission between that and San Diego. San Antonio and San Luís Obispo should be established in the north, and explorations should be made with the idea of starting new missions in the San Francisco Bay area. Agricultural tools were in the hold of the ship, as well as church goods and all the necessary supplies required for the new missions. Gálvez had backed up his commands with men, implements, tools, seeds and livestock.

In accordance with his directions, Fr. Serra assigned each of the new missionaries to his post. Frs. Pieras and Sitjar, both from Majorca, were to go to San Antonio; Frs. Juncosa and Cavaller to San Luís Obispo; Frs. Cruzado and Paterna to San Buenaventura; Frs. Cambón and Somera to San Gabriel; Frs. Dumetz and Jayme, also Majorcans, were to replace Frs. Parrón and Gómez, who were ill and had asked permission to return to Mexico. Fages countersigned the assignments, giving his official seal of approval, then the documents were sent to Verger and Gálvez, accompanied by a personal letter to each from Serra.

To Verger, Serra's words were humble but insistent. Still more priests were needed, and he stressed the necessity of dependable and accelerated supply lines between Mexico and California. The new land was producing, but so far, barely enough for survival. Staples, hard goods, manufactured products must come from Mexico. The ships were slow and the sailings dangerously far apart.

Serra urged Gálvez' continued support. Gálvez understood the problems of the missions, perhaps better than anyone else outside of California, and Serra could speak to him in confidence. Of himself, he wrote, "Would that it will not be less than I promise myself and the more I fear doing less, the greater is my desire to accomplish more." [2]

As soon as her vital cargo had been unloaded, the *San Antonio* weighed anchor and set sail for San Diego. Fages and the missionaries assigned to the southern missions were aboard. Before Fages left, Serra had prevailed upon a favorable mood and had obtained permission to found Mission San Antonio during his absence.

The sails disappeared over the horizon. The next morning, July 8, 1771, right after saying the Mass, Serra set out with Frs. Pieras and Sitjar, seven soldiers, nine cows, two heifers and a bull, six calves, a sow, a boar, a hen and chicks and eight mules. On the backs of the mules were packed flour, chocolate, plows, seeds, candles, vestments, chalices, bells...all the necessary items for the embryo settlement.

Traveling southwest, through the Santa Lucía Mountains, the missionary party came to a pleasant, wooded valley, which they named *Cañada de los Robles,* Valley of the Oaks. The warm, penetrating valley sunshine was a welcome reward after long months in the cooler coastal climate of Monterey. Serra selected a spot which, to all appearances seemed suitable for a mission. A lively stream ran through the green valley. High grass and vegetation indicated fertile soil.

The cross was raised and the bells were rung in the branches of a great oak tree, in preparation for the

---

2. Geiger, *op. cit.*, Vol. I, p. 276.

founding of Alta California's third mission. This was a moment of triumph, of hope—a moment apart from the frustrations, confinements and limitations that had held Serra captive the last two years; a moment under a warm July sun, a moment of uninhibited freedom.

The bells rang out, loud and clear—their metallic song undulating, reverberating through the awesome, empty silence—the silence of a primordial, virginal land. Serra's spirit, all of his freedom-loving heritage, his natural energy, his apostolic zeal, his vocational dedication to the love of Christ seemed to soar into one penetrating, clarion call. Chiming with the clear rhythm of the bells, his sonorous voice, like a canticle, called out to all who might hear them, to all who would come in the years following, "Come...come to the holy Church, come, come to receive the faith of Jesus Christ!"[3]

The dedication ceremony that July 14, 1771, was much as usual, with one difference. During the sermon, Serra had noticed a single Indian standing on a hill some distance away, watching the proceedings. After the ceremonies Serra approached the native, offered him gifts and showed in sign language that the priests and Spaniards wanted to be friends. The Indian left stoically but later returned with others of his tribe. They brought gifts for the strangers and Mission San Antonio seemed to be off to a good start.

Serra stayed on at the new mission for two weeks, helping with the work of building and acquainting the padres with their new tasks. They must begin immediately to learn the native language and in the meantime accept the little mannerisms that would lead to friendship with a people whose life was completely foreign to their own. They would accept the ways of the native,

---

3. Geiger, *op. cit.*, Vol. I, p. 280.

not force theirs on him. They would eat his food and work beside him. They would sing with him, pray with him and live with him, not as strangers, but as one of his own. With keen awareness of the natives' needs, capabilities and shortcomings, the priests would relate to native customs, habits, and ideas, fostering some and gradually eliminating others.

When the San Antonio fathers were securely sheltered in their temporary buildings, Serra returned to Monterey, leaving most of the military to guard the new mission. In Monterey, he quickly assembled a group of workers and went to Carmel to start work on Mission San Carlos de Borromeo de Carmelo, which would be his home mission from that time on.

For six busy months he worked with the few soldiers and workmen on hand along with the natives, clearing and leveling ground, cutting, hauling and nailing timbers into place, and thatching roofs. Relieved of Fages' nagging and autocratic rule, the soldiers worked diligently and cheerfully. Soon the work was done. Buildings took definite form and so did the missionary spirit. At every opportunity Serra talked to the natives, encouraging their friendship. Gradually he built the foundation and nucleus of a productive mission. On August 24, 1771, he blessed the cross and sang the high Mass of dedication.

But in southern California things were not going so well. Fages and the missionaries assigned to founding the new missions there had disembarked from the *San Antonio* at San Diego. Rivera, too, had come up from Baja with the soldiers commissioned for the founding of the new missions. Fages now had fifty men under his command. Everything was as Gálvez had planned. There was no reason to postpone the overdue San Buenaventura. The missionaries were eager to go. It had been arranged that they would meet Serra at the site for the dedication. The arrangement agreed upon before the *San Antonio* had left Monterey included that Fages would send a military escort to Monterey for Serra's land trip to San Buenaventura. No escort was sent. Instead, Fages kept his entire military group at San Diego. This first of the California mission string had not recovered from its inherent difficulties.

On the brighter side, many natives had turned in trust and friendship to the padres: conversions had increased; baptisms and marriages were regularly performed; the most reliable families and workers had moved into the compound; the regular routine of missionary life was progressing.

But by contrast, hundreds of Indians were still living in their original villages some distance from the mission. These were the thieving and mischievous natives whom the Spaniards had first encountered. Indian converts from the compound had made regular visits to the native villages in a feeble attempt to teach Christianity. This arrangement had never been approved by Serra and was totally unproductive. In fact, the very sight of their brothers receiving gifts and food from the missionaries in reward for their work infuriated the outland Indians and further stimulated bad feelings.

Moreover, the mission Indians were far from enjoying prosperity. The land surrounding the mission was poor. The water supply was inconstant. Crops had not been abundant. Food and supplies had been stretched to the utmost when the "invasion" came.

Rivera with all his men, Fages, and the new missionaries all descended on the poor little mission struggling for sustenance. Word was sent to Monterey and that unit shared its dwindling provisions with San Diego.

The two San Diego priests, Frs. Gómez and Parrón, were ill and waiting to return to Mexico. They welcomed their successors, Frs. Dumetz and Jayme.

Frs. Paterna and Cruzado, assigned to San Buenaventura, had no choice but to await Fages' signal to go ahead, a signal which did not come. Reluctantly, however, he did agree that Frs. Cambón and Somera might proceed with plans for the establishment of San Gabriel. He would not go with them. The two priests, accordingly, hustled around, assembling supplies, and finally on August 6, 1771, the four muleteers packed their reliable beasts of burden and with a ten-man military guard and corporal, the two padres mounted and rode off into the north.

For nine days they plodded mile after mile along the dusty Portolá trail, civilization's only connecting thread. Then, on a quiet afternoon, they relaxed military formation to rest in a pleasant valley.

Suddenly, shattering the silence, a screaming, yelping, painted mob of Indians, armed with bows and arrows, rushed toward them. The soldiers scrambled for their guns. Straight and tall, one of the priests calmly walked toward the fiery natives and unrolled a large, realistic picture of Our Lady of Sorrows. The Indians stopped still before the painting and dropped their weapons. The chiefs laid gifts of beads before the likeness and made signs of reverence, indicating an intention of peace and friendship. They even sent for other natives from neighboring villages. The Spaniards graciously accepted this abrupt change of attitude and reciprocated with kindly gestures and gifts, as substantial proof that their intentions also were entirely peaceful. Then they moved on toward their destination.

There was no mistaking the San Miguel Valley, so clearly and minutely described as a suitable spot for a mission. In fact, Crespí's diary so specifically describes landmarks that even today, historians can retrace the steps of these early pioneers through a maze of freeways and city skyscrapers. With a backdrop of precipitous blue mountains on the east, it was indeed a rich, fertile valley, crossed by two rivers. Trees of many kinds and tall grass, now brown in the autumn sun, covered the plain which gradually sloped down to the water's edge. Wild berries and grapes roused visions of future fruit orchards and nut groves. The padres' wildest imaginings, however, could not have perceived that this embryonic core of western civilization, this tranquil, silent valley, would one day be surrounded by one of the greatest cities of the world—Los Angeles.

Visitors from all parts of the world today are fascinated by the magnificent San Gabriel Mission, moved in 1775 to its present site. Later known as the "Queen of the Missions,"[4] its venerable facade, famous campanile and wealth of artifacts are devoutly preserved by the Claretian Fathers, who maintain it as a parish church. San Gabriel, a thriving, residential city, still maintains a quiet charm, reminiscent of the past, despite its proximity to the rushing, surging buzz of freeway traffic. Its mountains and river preserve the original name the padres gave this early mission site.

On September 8, 1771, Frs. Cambón and Somera erected the cross and said the Mass of dedication. The next day building began, with unexpected assistance. The Indians came, mingled with the soldiers and eagerly offered to help with the work. No doubt the workmen considered the unsolicited apprentices more of a hindrance than a help, but the more patient padres

---

4. This term has also been applied to Mission Santa Barbara. Both were most productive and beautiful architectural specimens. Santa Barbara was founded after Fr. Serra's time.

accepted this further gesture of good will as a favorable portent and directed their untrained energy into useful channels. In record time the temporary church and the house for the priests were finished. The presidio and corral soon followed, all enclosed by the usual stockade.

Unfortunately, the beneficent beginning was soon blighted. The Indians came in droves, delighting the padres, but the military took a dim view of this inundation of a disorderly mob. In fact, the corporal was terrified, and his fear became the cause of the violence he dreaded. He gave orders that no more than five Indians should be admitted inside the compound at one time.

With a jolt, the senseless order not only halted but contradicted all that the padres had come to accomplish. Furthermore, the Indians regarded this as a contemptuous insult. They had built the mission. It was theirs. They had shown goodwill toward the white man, and he had repaid them with dishonor. The padres pleaded with the corporal, but to no avail.

About this time Fages arrived from San Diego on an inspection trip. The padres presented their case and he assented. The natives, by all means, must be allowed inside the stockade. Otherwise, how could they receive instruction and training? Fages' hearty agreement with the padres, however, was pure histrionics. As he left the compound, he whispered orders to the corporal not to allow a single Indian inside the stockade.

It was a typical Fages doublecross; an arbitrary usurpation of military power; disrespect for the authority of the padres; a defiant contradiction of the missionary effort he had been commissioned to promote. As a result, the padres, bottled up in the compound, were exiled from the natives and the natives outside were deprived of the missionary leadership they had encouraged and welcomed.

Whether purposely or by accident, Fages had placed in command of the San Gabriel military unit a man of weak and immoral character. Fages had never shown any particular objection to the fraternization of his men with the Indians. In fact, there were times when he seemed to encourage it, if straying to Indian huts meant fewer men to feed in camp. This had always been one of the serious sources of conflict between Fages and the missionaries. Regulations absolutely forbade immoral association of the military with native women. Such acts were to be judged and punished by the padres. But Fages allowed the priests no authority over the military, and despite Serra's insistence on strict moral conduct, Fages was inclined to overlook the incidents or to deal indulgently with the offenders.

At San Gabriel, the problem was climaxed when one of the soldiers molested the wife of the chief. All evidence pointed to the corporal himself.

One afternoon the soldiers were going about their daily routine of rounding up the horses outside the stockade, when suddenly Indians appeared from everywhere. The little group of Spaniards, taken totally by surprise, ran for their leather jackets and guns, but before they could get organized, the mob of angry, painted natives armed with bows and arrows had surrounded them. Without waiting for a sign of peace or parley, the corporal pulled a gun and aimed. A shot rang out and the chief fell to the ground, dead. The other Indians fled.

This was not enough. The soldiers cut the head from the corpse and hung it from a pole, using the excuse that the gory sight would frighten the natives into submission. Eight of the soldiers followed the Indians as they fled, disarmed them and returned to camp. The horrified padres demanded that the head be immediately removed from the pole, but the repugnance of the heinous act lived on.

The next day, October 11, the entire horizon was a circle of fire. All the villages of the area had united in a signal, but unbelievably a signal of peace. Most of the California Indians were actually peaceful peoples. Seemingly aware of division between the military and the missionaries, they cast their reliance on the padres' denunciation of the soldiers' misbehavior and violence and offered to make peace.

Again in late October, Fages came by San Gabriel. With him this time were Frs. Paterna and Cruzado with the military guard assigned for the founding of the long postponed mission San Buenaventura. The lurid details of San Gabriel's "Indian hostilities" were colorfully expounded.

This news Fages hailed as factual justification for his past behavior. With the superiority of one who knew it all the time, he declared, "Now San Buenaventura cannot be founded, nor indeed, San Luís Obispo, because I need the soldiers to reinforce this mission as well as San Antonio."[5] He left six more men at San Gabriel—a total of eighteen men with nothing to do.

Actually, the corporal in charge at San Gabriel had been the source of all the trouble. When Serra heard of the situation, he sent the trustworthy Corporal Joseph María Góngora from Carmel to take charge. Immediately the scene changed. Repairs and improvements were made to buildings; the natives resumed their contact with the missionaries and learned the usual arts of cultivation and building.

Everyone agreed that the San Gabriel natives were very different from all the other California groups. Left to go ahead in peace, despite the darkened beginnings, San Gabriel became one of the most successful and productive missions of the entire chain.

Fages continued on toward Monterey. On the way, as he had promised at San Gabriel, he left more men at San Antonio. But he placed a corporal over them who was of much the same stamp as the first one in San Gabriel. The men refused to work, just loafed around. This situation resulted in more mouths to feed and no one to do the work. The padres and Indians turned carpenters, livestock keepers, muleteers and soldiers.

Fages arrived in Monterey with the rest of the men, cattle, mules and bad news. Admittedly, Fages had problems. The additional men Rivera had recruited from Baja for military service in Alta California were of extremely low caliber. Many had been prisoners. As soon as they had arrived in San Diego, they had begun to desert, some retracing their steps to Baja, others running off to the Indian camps. Those who stayed refused to work or loafed on the job. To have to rely on such a weak defense for the new missions was, to say the least, discouraging.

Still, Fages' management of the men was responsible for most of the resentment and distrust among military ranks. He would order severe and unjust punishment for minor military infractions, while overlooking or actually encouraging immoral conduct. This along with his natural stubbornness and resentment of Serra's authority created a depressing situation. The thin line of defense gradually weakened. Animosity among the natives grew. They rightfully demanded reparation for Spanish abuses of their women. Particularly repugnant to the padres was the deplorable reality that so called Christian Spaniards were flauntingly breaking the very laws, ideals and customs the padres had come to instill among the natives.

To the zealous and dynamic Serra, the trouble at San Gabriel was distressing enough; the news that Fages had interfered with the founding of San Gabriel was distressing enough, but the news that Fages had halted the founding of San Buenaventura again and refused to go ahead with San Luís Obispo was tragic. Waiting, frustration, defiance—Serra's cross far exceeded that of physical pain.

Despite all hindrances, Carmel was making progress. Great numbers of converts were receiving baptism, but the regular mission schedule was hindered by lack of supplies, complications of distances, delay in communications, government interference and mostly by Fages.

Ignoring Fages' declaration at San Gabriel, Serra requested him to supply the six soldiers necessary for founding San Luís Obispo. Again, even with thirty-six soldiers idle at Monterey, Fages refused. He made one concession, however. Serra had been pushing for the exploration of San Francisco Bay with the idea of determining favorable locations for the two proposed missions in that area.

On March 25, 1772, Fages, accompanied by the usual military and Fr. Crespí, as diarist and chaplain, set out to explore the San Francisco Bay region. They scouted along the seemingly endless, irregular shoreline of the great waterway for miles, reaching the east bay side and as far north as the outlet of the San Joaquin and Sacramento Rivers, at what is now Carquinez Straight. Amazed at the bay's extent, they concluded that it was impossible for a land party to reach the north shore, and that further exploration should be done by ship.

While they were still reconnoitering the inlets and tributaries of the vast San Francisco Bay, word came of serious famine in San Gabriel. When the northern missions had shared their meager allotment of supplies with San Diego in July, they had been left dangerously short. In fact, every mission in Alta California was in dire need of food and supplies, but San Gabriel was faced with starvation and revolt.

Gálvez had planned that nine shipments of supplies and goods would arrive in California between 1769 and 1771. Due to disasters at sea, scurvy and a shortage of ships, four had arrived. It had been a year now since the *San Antonio's* last voyage and the number of hungry mouths had multiplied.

Fages hastily returned to Monterey, organized a group of his best marksmen and started out for the "Cañada de los Osos," "Valley of the Bears," proposed site of Mission San Luís Obispo. The expedition was successful. The soldiers shot about thirty bears, dried the meat and distributed it among the missions most in need. The hunt also paid an unexpected dividend. The wild bears had been the age-old enemy of the defenseless natives. By exterminating the dreaded beasts, the Spaniards had won the lasting friendship of the San Luís Obispo Indians.

Seeds, milk and bear jerky managed to sustain life, but privation lasted into the summer of 1772. In August of that year, word came that the *San Carlos* and *San Antonio* were both anchored in San Diego harbor. *San Antonio's* orders were to sail on to Monterey, but treacherous head winds in the Santa Barbara channel had forced her back to the southern port. Captain Pérez, no less daring in 1772 than he had been in 1769, captained a ship that had not been too sturdy when new. Now her timbers shivered with age and strain and his best judgment was to turn back. Serra wrote Palóu, "Now we have everything in San Diego and nothing here." [6] There was no choice: they must bring the supplies from San Diego by mule train—a long, slow, tedious task.

Due to Serra's persistence and persuasive powers, Fages finally yielded. San Luís Obispo could be founded during the journey south to retrieve the provisions.

Accordingly, on August 24, 1772, Serra, Fages, Fr. Caveller, who had been assigned to the San Luís Mission, and a ten-year-old Indian boy, whom Serra had baptized, started south with a group of soldiers and muleteers.

On the first day of September, 1772, Serra blessed the cross and said the Mass for the founding of the fifth mission of the chain, San Luís Obispo. Then they hurried on, leaving Fr. Caveller there alone with eight soldiers and a drastically meager bundle of supplies. More supplies had been promised and Fr. Juncosa was to come later with a corporal of the guard and four additional men. The bear hunt had opened the door for a friendly reception, and Fr. Caveller began the usual building and teaching.

Serra had never before seen the Santa Barbara Channel Indians. He had heard Crespí, Fages, Portolá, Pérez and others tell of great numbers of tall, sturdy natives of exceptionally good physique. Now, he saw them and perceived beyond all his former aspirations the compelling need for missions among these fine people. Thousands lived in the twenty Chumash villages—friendly, imaginative, active human beings waiting and ready for the teaching and uplifting leader-

---

6. Tibesar, Vol. I, p. 265.

ship of the missionaries. Serra speculated that at least three missions were needed in the area. To see these people was to love them with the boundless love of his apostolic heart, and he longed now more than ever before to bring them the love and the faith of Christ.

They pushed on to San Gabriel, the only mission Serra had not seen. Frs. Cambón and Somera seemed to have overcome the dismal events of their beginning and things were going well. This tribe was distinct from all the others, but seemed cooperative, and eager to learn, work and become Christians. As Serra's arms reached out to them with gifts, his prayers reached to heaven on their behalf. In the close relationship of prayer and sacrifice, these were his own. He congratulated the priests and reported to his superiors that this was, "without doubt the most excellent mission site so far discovered."[7]

But San Gabriel still seemed to be the victim of some sort of military imbroglio. Serra learned from the priests that Fages had given secret orders to remove the respected Corporal Góngora and replace him with the previous disreputable corporal who had caused so much trouble in the beginning. He went directly to Fages, who denied all knowledge of the matter. However, a letter in Serra's possession established undeniable proof and Fages finally admitted guilt and promised to allow Góngora to remain at San Gabriel.

The missionary president's duties extended from the exalted heights of offering the holy Sacrifice of the Mass to the detection of the devious schemes of degraded corporals.

They left San Gabriel secure and peaceful for the moment and continued on to San Diego. It was a fast trip, considering the usual speed of a mule train. For

---

7. *Ibid.,* p. 359.

one thing, the animals carried no burden, and for another, Fages was really a man of action with the ability to move forward when it was in his interest to do so.

Memories undoubtedly crowded Serra's mind of those first tragic days in San Diego as he compared the fragile beginning with the thriving settlement of 1772, now a busy rendezvous for ships, laymen and priests. Serra talked a bit with Frs. Crespí and Dumetz, who were there temporarily before going on to Monterey, and with the two mission priests, Frs. Jayme and Tomás de la Pena.

Then he went to see Pérez and to persuade him to sail the *San Antonio* on to Monterey. He emphasized the desperate and immediate need in Monterey and the other northern missions. Mule trains were slow, awkward and limited to carrying smaller cargo. Bulky articles needed for agriculture and the churches must be transported by other means. Pérez knowledge of the northern seas and the fact that winter was coming on had convinced him it was not wise. Yet, Serra's personality, his zeal, and his irrefutable arguments finally moved the captain to agree to the northern trip. The *San Antonio* not only reached Monterey safely, but returned to San Blas without mishap. Another crisis had passed and the northern missions had been saved.

Serra's next undertaking was to persuade Fages to agree to the founding of San Buenaventura. Here he was not so successful. Fages not only refused to consider the project, but was holding in his possession both outgoing and incoming mail containing orders and information of the utmost importance.

This was the last straw: Fages had stifled, restricted and strangled the missionary development. All the padres agreed that the enterprise was doomed with Fages in California. They urged Serra to go to Mexico and state his case before the viceroy.

De Croix was no longer viceroy, but Bucareli, his replacement, who had just arrived from Spain, was a zealous, sincere man of responsibility. He had heard there were strained relations between the military and religious in California, and he was deeply concerned about the California project. Gálvez had returned to Madrid because of illness. However, he still held an important post high in government circles and followed fervently and enthusiastically all news of the missions he had so expeditiously begun.

It was the right moment for Serra to go to Mexico. The missions had reached a deadend. Portolá's warning to Fages to remember that the primary purpose of the Alta California conquest was to extend the faith had not only been ignored; it had been rejected. Now, the project lay paralyzed. Its revival and continuance depended on the success or failure of Serra's interview with the viceroy in Mexico.

Always Go Forward

Serra's trip to San Diego, his insistence that Pérez sail on to Monterey and the subsequent arrival of the *San Antonio* had saved the northern missions. Monterey had survived the crisis of 1772, but survival was not enough. The mission system, still in its infancy, must grow and move forward or die. Serra knew that Fages' autocratic control, his refusal to move ahead at this crucial time threatened the entire system. The outcome of his trip to Mexico would decide the fate of the Alta California missions. In fact, his very determination to go had immediate effects.

Not until Serra boarded the *San Carlos* and sailed out of San Diego Bay on October 29, 1772, did Fages realize, to his horror, the weakness of his own position. He, the commander, now stood powerless before the humble, limping Franciscan. The gray-frocked "visionary" had suddenly become a political entity, a power in the echelons of government. As the white sails faded over the horizon, Fages knew that he himself was but a figurehead, disgraced, chastised, bereft of command.

He began to change. His blustering attitude vanished. He appeared more generous, more tolerant, more sympathetic toward the padres and his own men.

The *San Carlos* made a fast trip to San Blas, arriving on November 4. Between San Blas and Mexico City, however, Serra must make a long, painstaking overland journey through miles of flat, barren lands, steaming jungles and steep, narrow mountain roads. Franciscan monasteries at intervals along the way would provide pleasant and friendly hospitality.

His first stop was in Tepic. Here Serra heard great news. The Dominican Order was taking over all Baja California missions. Fr. Palóu and his Franciscans were free for service elsewhere. Serra wrote Palóu, hoping soon they would be together in California. This was more than a hope. Due to communication gaps, Serra could not know that Verger had appointed Palóu and six of his fellow missionaries to Alta and that at the moment Serra was writing his letter, they were enroute to Monterey.

Juan Bautista, a bright, young Indian boy, loyal and helpful to Serra, was making the trip with him. It was a great adventure for the boy, but somewhere along the way, no doubt in the mosquito infested jungle, both Juan and Serra contracted fever.

When they arrived at the monastery in Guadalupe, the two travelers were desperately ill. Certain that death was imminent, the friars administered the last sacraments. As the burning fever tortuously enervated his sixty-year-old body, Serra prayed for Juan. He was not only concerned about the boy's welfare, for he had become very fond of him, but he was fearful of the effects at home, should the boy die. He knew that in the minds of the parents and indeed the entire tribe, no possible explanation could ever remove the belief that the Spaniards had deliberately captured the boy with the intention of killing him. Juan's death could mean an entire Indian colony's rejection of everything Christian.

The boy recovered, no doubt due to Serra's prayers. Serra's fever subsided and despite the pleas and warnings of the friars, he was determined to continue his journey. Serra had never spared himself, and he had work to do. He must go forward—never turn back.

It was an arduous trip, even for a younger, stronger man. When Serra reached Querétaro, the fever again raged and his relapse became extremely serious. There seemed no doubt now that his death was but a matter of hours or days away. Serra prepared to meet his God, but prayed that he might finish this last task and return to Monterey. Eventually, the fever left his enfeebled body. He was spared, but the illness had delayed his journey by several weeks. It was on February 6, 1773, that he and Juan arrived at the College of San Fernando in Mexico City.

After the long, grueling journey, Serra, weak and wan, found security and solace in the well-ordered monastic life. Re-entering the intellectual and cultural atmosphere of this center of spirituality was like coming home to a world far removed from the rugged frontier life of California. Indeed, San Fernando had been his New World home for a large part of the last twenty-four years. It had been his destination when he left Majorca. Again, San Fernando had been his headquarters after he left Sierra Gorda, and during the several years he had spent in Mexico preaching and teaching. He found friends there and memories. Fr. Verger, fellow Majorcan and confrere, welcomed the president of the California missions with reverence and respect. They reminisced over the difficulties of a Majorcan's gaining recognition in the foreign missionary field in 1749. Now, twenty-four years later, Verger was guardian of the leading Franciscan missionary college in New Spain; Serra, Palóu and Crespí held important posts in California; and Majorcan Franciscans made up a large percentage of the entire New World missionary personnel.

Juan's eyes opened wide, as he looked, listened and observed strange sights and sounds of a world he never could have imagined. He was amazed by the great buildings and rushing crowds of the city, but he was especially surprised to see Spanish women. No white women had come to California. Now he knew these Spaniards had mothers, wives and sisters just as his own people did. Spaniards were not born of mules, as some Indians had concluded. Juan also found enough familiar sights and sounds in the strange land to feel comfortable. The churches, though more majestic, had bells that sounded much like those of the missions, and gray-robed friars spoke in the same quiet, friendly manner. As he had done at home, Juan spent the days helping Serra and praying, working and singing with the friars.

Serra's appetite and physical energy were slow to return. But his determination to pursue the object of his trip had not diminished. The friars pleaded with him to rest a few months, to wait until his strength returned, until he was refreshed in mind and body. But Serra held tenaciously to the accomplishment of his mission. To Verger, he reported in detail the events, activities, results, plight and dilemma of the Alta California mission. He outlined his program of changes and adjustments, his hopes and his plans. Verger, whose letters may have sounded stolidly pragmatic and unimaginative, was zealously devoted to the missionary ideal. He understood Serra's problems, approved the entire program and urged Serra to see Bucareli as soon as possible.

The rugged years of frontier life had not diminished Serra's polished diplomatic acumen, his charm and ready wit. Nor had they dulled those brilliant persuasive powers for which he was noted in Palma, in Mexico City and in California. His conferences with Antonio María Bucareli Ursua, gentleman from the courts of Madrid and newly appointed viceroy of New Spain, took place in the splendor of the royal palace of Mexico City in March.

A devout Christian, Bucareli was totally sympathetic with the missionary project of California. Judging from the disturbing rumors he had heard and the confusing official letters he had received from Fages, he had concluded that much should be set right and was eager to know the real facts. Serra's direct and impartial truthfulness matched his zeal, his enthusiasm and his practical knowledge of affairs. The viceroy was impressed by his effectual suggestions and wise judgment. He gave the padre sufficient time to state his case. The conferences were not only congenial, but also fruitful, both for the government and for the missions.

Their first consideration was California's lifeline. Men, animals and missions require food and other necessities. Since no overland routes had been established, the sea lanes to Monterey and San Diego were of vital importance and the number of ships and sailings had to be increased to keep the struggling missions alive through the critical initial years.

Bucareli had been advised that the port of San Blas was badly situated. Its needed improvements would be too costly; it had never been and never would be a

suitable harbor. Upon this advice he had all but decided to abandon it. Serra attempted to convince the
viceroy that without San Blas, California would become
an orphan, with no communication, no source of supply. Serra's first victory was Bucareli's agreement to
maintain San Blas, at least for the present.

Because San Blas was not an ideal harbor and the
sea lanes alone could not support the growing needs of
the new colony, Serra accentuated the importance of
opening land routes to California. This was not a new
idea. Gálvez had launched the California project on this
premise. Spanish soldiers had died in Sonora Indian
wars that this might be accomplished. It had been the
topic of conversation and conferences in government
and military circles for years. But no definite action had
been taken.

Serra reminded the viceroy that Indian relations
were particularly favorable at this time and that Captain Juan Bautista de Anza, commander of the presidio
at Tubac, would be a most able leader for an overland
expedition. He stressed the importance of government
financing and the issuance of authoritative orders for
the establishment of an overland route from Sonora to
Monterey.

The viceroy assured Serra of his cooperation in
these and all other matters discussed and asked that
Serra put his ideas and requests in writing. This Serra
gladly did.

Back in the seclusion of San Fernando he worked
resolutely, spelling out point-by-point in thirty-two well
defined legal terms the specific rights of the Indians
and the duties, responsibilities, privileges and restrictions of the soldiers, including the punishment to be
administered for transgression. He recommended that
one hundred men be sent to California immediately,

that the soldiers' pay be increased, and that special inducements be given to married men who wished to become permanent residents.

He defined the duties, restrictions and qualifications of military men, post-office officials, missionaries and colonists, even stating the personal characteristics necessary for the governor of the frontier missionary project. Serra's *Representación* had all the aspects of important legal documents prepared by Spain's best attorneys at law. The limping padre from California had demonstrated a new qualification not before observed.

Signed on March 13, 1773, the *Representación* became the "Constitution" of the missionary movement from that time on. All government officials and all missionaries were bound to abide by it. Bucareli's recommendation to the viceregal council that it be ratified in its entirety was accepted. Later, the document was signed and approved by the king.

This marked the coming-of-age of the California project. The missionary movement was no longer an experiment, a dream. It had acquired legal status; all points of procedure were now specifically defined. The movement had won the respectful attention and regard of Spanish officials as a permanent and valuable entity in the Spanish Empire.

Serra had achieved the fundamental purpose of his journey, the vital point that "the government control and education of the baptized Indians should belong exclusively to the missionaries."[1]

Rooted in Christian doctrine and nourished by its charity, the missions could advance only under religious leadership. Without spiritual motivation they

---

1. *Decree of Bucareli and Council*, Mexico, May 6, 1773.

could degenerate into military fortresses or government slave camps. Serra felt that to have obtained an irrefutable, legally formalized statement on this vital issue alone merited his long, painful, hazardous trip.

Grateful for a successful outcome of his earnest pilgrimage, the weak and pale, sixty-year-old padre and his eager Indian companion, Juan, prepared for their homeward journey. The San Fernando fathers attempted to persuade Serra to stay for a time. He needed to recuperate and they needed him. They even wanted to elect him guardian of San Fernando. Indicative of their regard for him is the following letter, written by Fr. Pablo Font, of the College of San Fernando, in August, 1773:

"The Father-president Junípero Serra is a religious of the observant order, a man of very venerable age, formerly professor at the University of Palma, who during twenty-four years, since he has been a missionary of this college, has never spared himself in toiling for the conversion of the faithful and the unfaithful. Notwithstanding his many and laborious years, he has the qualities of a lion, which surrenders only to fever. Neither the habitual indispositions from which he suffers, especially in the chest and in difficulty of breathing, nor the wounds in his feet and legs have been able to detain him a moment from his apostolic tasks. He had astonished us during his recent sojourn, for, although very sick, he never failed, day or night, to take part in the choir, much less when he had fever. We have seen him apparently dead, only to be almost immediately revived. If now and then he attended to the needs of bodily health at the infirmary, it was only because he was ordered to go there. Sometimes, in his journeys among the faithful and the unfaithful he has become so ill, on account of wounds and other infirmities, that it was necessary to carry him on a stretcher, but he did not wish to stop to cure his half-dead body, and soon he would be restored to health, through the influence of Divine Providence alone.

"In truth, on account of these things, and because of the austerity of his life, his humility, charity, and other virtues, he now is returning, as if it were nothing, to Monterey, a distance of a thousand leagues by sea and land, to visit those missions and rejoice them by his presence and by the measures which he had procured and to preside over them and found other missions until he shall die. May God grant him many years of life. Much more could I say of this holy man. He has at various times been elected Father superior, but was never confirmed, either on account of his absence or because the prelates thought it wiser not to withdraw such an extraordinary man from his apostolic tasks."[2]

Appreciative of his brothers' concern and affection, but still more certain of his destiny, Serra could give no consideration to lingering in an atmosphere of esteem and ease. He wanted only to return to his people, to be of service to them, and to be among them as quickly as possible. The Indians of California needed him far more than did his Franciscan brothers in Mexico City.

Pérez, former captain of the *San Antonio* and Serra's good friend, had been given command of a new frigate, the *Santiago,* which was scheduled to sail on her maiden voyage in January of the new year. The padre and Juan retraced their treacherous overland path to San Blas, where they boarded the *Santiago.* They arrived safely in San Diego in March, 1774.

Once again the sight of white sails on San Diego's horizon signified restoration of life for the Alta Califor-

---

2. Chapman, *History of California, The Spanish Period,* p. 358.

nia missions. Hunger in varying degrees had been the missions' companion from the beginning. Crops had matured in the new land, but because of increased demands, the supply problem continued to be serious.

The *Santiago's* arrival meant not only a fresh and bountiful stock of food; it meant the coming of desperately needed personnel: a doctor, artisans, skilled tradesmen and the first white women and children to step on California soil. So, the coming of the *Santiago* marked the transition of status. California was no longer a frontier camp. It was now a Spanish settlement.

Deeply stirred to have safely returned to San Diego, Serra took time to evaluate conditions there and to discuss immediate problems with his good friends and fellow Majorcans, Fr. Jayme and Fr. Fuster. Then he continued overland, on to Carmel, stopping at each mission along the way. He noted remarkable progress everywhere. The natives, who had had no agricultural background in their thousands of years of existence, were now beginning to learn the delicate art of stirring the earth to produce food. In the warmth of the sun, seeds were sprouting and the earth, carpeted in its brilliant, new green, gave promise of another budding spring.

Palóu was at Monterey when Serra came home on May 11. As the two good friends embraced, each remembered Serra's farewell at Baja, "until we meet in Monterey."[3] The *Santiago*, like a homing pigeon, was riding at anchor in Monterey Bay, and the warehouses were filled with supplies from her hold.

Palóu and six of the Baja Franciscans had arrived seven months before. Verger had suggested Palóu take charge of the missions until Serra's return. Fages had

---

3. Geiger, *op. cit.*, Vol. I, p. 62.

mellowed and worked with Palóu to keep things working smoothly, as Serra had observed on his trip home from San Diego.

The results of Serra's mission to Mexico City followed closely behind him. Twelve days after his homecoming, he greeted the new military commander, Fernando Rivera y Moncada. California was no stranger to Rivera, nor was he a stranger to Californians. This was the same Rivera who had led the second land expedition to California in 1769 and who, again, had brought men and livestock up from Baja in 1771. Serra had first met the lieutenant as commander in charge of mission property under Portolá in Baja during the interim between the Jesuit exodus and the Franciscan arrival. This relationship had little to recommend him.

Nor was Rivera pleased over his California assignment. He had hoped to retire because he was not well, and had settled down in a chosen Baja location, where he had bought a new home. All his money was invested in this venture. His family had no desire to move to the raw frontier and Rivera's financial condition was negative. He was forced to borrow the money for transportation. Nonetheless, a military man obeys orders and when Bucareli requested that he go to California to replace Fages, he promptly complied. Fages quietly rode off to San Diego, where he sailed on the *San Antonio* to San Blas.

Rivera had claimed admiration for the missionary movement, but actually was not in favor of any part of it. Concerned with his own comfort and ease, he resented his appointment to California. He had flatly refused to consider the founding of new missions. Despite Serra's persuasion and direct orders from Bucareli that he should proceed immediately with the long delayed San Buenaventura and the new San Francisco missions, nothing was done.

"What are we doing here, since it is plain that with this man in charge, no new mission will ever be established?"[4] lamented Serra. His hands were tied. Furthermore, Rivera refused to carry out the rules of the *Representación,* or to cooperate with the missionary fathers. Since the day that Portolá had sailed out of Monterey Bay, the missions had been beset with obstinate, recalcitrant military commanders; men who regarded the Indian as a troublesome, dirty, worthless savage, and who had little sympathy with the idea of christianizing him.

In the face of all handicaps, there was no denying the progress and the growth of the missions. They had taken root. No one man could stop their development. He might bind the branches and prune the main limbs, but the missions had been solidly established in California. By this time, a mutually intuitive understanding between native and padre had evolved into a corporate determination and tenacity.

Men who had known hunger and the necessity of subsisting on whatever was available, were producing food for themselves and enjoying the felicity of a full stomach and well-stocked larder. There was an abundance of milk, and the women were learning to feed their children nourishing food and to keep them clean.

Serra was particularly concerned with the children. He wrote Bucareli: "The spectacle of seeing about a hundred young children of about the same age praying and answering individually all the questions asked on Christian doctrine, hearing them sing, seeing them go-

---

4. Tibesar, *Serra's Letter to Father Guardian,* Vol. II, p. 111.

ing about clothed in cotton and woolen garments, play-
ing happily and dealing with the padres so intimately as
if they had always known them, is indeed something
moving, a thing for which God is to be thanked."[5]

Serra longed to push it all ahead faster and farther.
But if progress had been slow, he could take comfort
from the knowledge that neither he nor the missions
were turning back. And portents and signs indicated
that Spanish enterprise was not yet dead.

Authorities in Madrid, worried about the encroachment of Russians along the northern shore, had ordered
Pérez to sail the *Santiago* as far north as the sixtieth
parallel, to examine the coast for possible foreign invasion, to chart the so-far-uncharted seas and to make
observations of the native life in that part of the new
territory.

The seasoned master mariner, well aware of the
hazards of such a voyage, made of Serra a sentimental
request. Would he say Mass under the famous Monterey Oak, first sanctified by Vizcaíno's three Carmelite
fathers in 1602, and again by Serra on June 3, 1770, in
the first Monterey Mass of the California expedition? It
was an hour of memories, especially for Crespí, Serra
and Pérez, and the others who had attended Serra's
first Mass there four years before, almost to the day.

Adverse winds and rough seas forced Pérez back at
the fifty-fifth parallel. But he had succeeded in planting
the Spanish flag on the island now known as Canada's
Queen Charlotte. He had charted the entire coastline;

---

5. Tibesar, *Serra's Letter to Bucareli*, August 24, 1774, Vol. II, p. 139.

he had made a complete and favorable report of the Indian tribes along the coast, whom he described as friendly; and he had seen no Russians. The assurance that California so far was not threatened by foreign powers was heartening news to Monterey, Mexico City and Madrid. Pérez and the *Santiago* safely arrived back in San Blas in November.

California
Comes of Age

The impact of Serra's conversations with Bucareli had penetrated far beyond the walls of Mexico City's royal palace. The pale, ailing padre, his eyes burning with earnest resolution, had convinced Bucareli of California's illimitable hopes.

Born of a sense of history and the vision of leadership, Serra's intelligent appraisals and his practical suggestions impressed Bucareli as both basically realistic and vitally important. Consequently, the viceroy informed Madrid that once rival European powers discovered the vast potential of this western empire, nationalistic aspirations would lead to aggression and belligerence.

Carlos III's orders to Gálvez to investigate possibilities for the occupation of California had issued from fear of Russian invasion. Now, Madrid began to send repeated warnings to Bucareli to secure the coast of California.

Pérez had assured the absence of foreign settlements as far north as the fifty-fifth parallel. But Bucareli was not satisfied. Suddenly the heretofore remote California missions were seen as a valuable political entity, and Spanish explorers again ventured on unknown seas.

Based upon Serra's evaluation of San Blas as a necessary base of operations, Spain's best naval officers were sent to transform the swampy, crumbling harbor into a safe, efficient and permanent port.

By the first of the new year, ships began to sail from the reconditioned naval base. The *San Antonio* once again sailed into San Diego Bay loaded with welcome supplies. The *San Carlos* followed in June. She stopped at Monterey but only long enough to unload supplies and mail. Bucareli had sent separate documents to Rivera and Serra containing specific instructions to establish two missions and a presidio in the San Francisco area without delay. Captain Juan Bautista de Ayala's orders were to sail the *San Carlos* into San Francisco Bay and to explore, survey and chart the entire area.

Approaching the narrow channel, now known as the Golden Gate, with extreme caution, Ayala lowered a small boat for reconnoitering. The boat was quickly swept into the bay by the incoming tide and the *San Carlos* followed.

The handsomely carved and decorated Spanish ship, riding high in the smooth water, its sails fluttering in a gentle breeze, seemed dwarfed by the magnitude of the inland sea. Even more impressive from the surface than from the hilltops above, calm, quiet, surrounded by low hills, the bay extended as far as they could see. Crespí had not exaggerated when he had said it would hold all the ships of Spain. Certainly it was a potential center of world trade and a providential spot for a great city.

Choosing as headquarters a large island, now known as Angel Island, they spent forty days reconnoitering, exploring, charting and mapping coves, inlets, small bays and the great river (Sacramento-San Joaquin) that pours into the harbor.

Plans had called for a rendezvous with Rivera and a land party, but Ayola and his men saw no signs of them. They did find a flag, cross and note left by Rivera and Fr. Palóu on an exploratory trip the year before. Then Ayala and the *San Carlos* returned to Monterey.

Meanwhile, Ecela, one of the officers of the *Santiago*, which had been exploring northern waters, was sufficiently interested in seeing the famed harbor from land to organize a party, which included Fr. Palóu. Following the route traveled by Rivera and Palóu the year before, they explored the shoreline and surrounding country. Rivera's adamant decision that it was not a suitable location for a mission or pueblo did not agree with their findings, nor, indeed, with those of any of the other groups that had visited the area. The Ecela party just missed the *San Carlos* but found papers left by the ship's officers and concluded, rightly, that they had returned to Monterey.

━━━━━━━━━━

Three Spanish ships lay at anchor in Monterey Bay at one time. This was an unprecedented event. Implicit to a ship is an aura of romance, and these three vessels had special significance. They bore testimony that no foreign power threatened their settlements; the ships, their officers and men were links with the world from which this group had long been separated; they directly represented the viceroy, who was commander, arbiter, ruler, and sole support; furthermore, they had come in the name of the king of Spain.

This called for celebrations! Everyone was in fiesta mood. Rivera banqueted the explorers with all the pomp, etiquette, splendor and courtly grace this far outpost would allow. Serra invited them to Carmel, where he spread his best table and generously entertained them with his typical affability, wit and charm. Fat beeves and lambs were slaughtered. Vegetables, fruit and berries were brought in from the gardens and fresh fish from the sea. Spirits were high and the men of the sea had tales to tell of their adventures and of the people they had seen while exploring northern coasts.

Serra was their most attentive listener. The natives were reported as friendly. The mission president sang the Mass of thanksgiving and transcendentally adopted those newly discovered people of the north. The same immutable urge that had sent him from Palma half-a-world across the sea, that same fire from within flared anew, not dimmed but fanned by age, hardship, discouragement and distance.

Serra spoke of planting missions all along the northern coast. Those friendly people were ready to learn trades, to build, to acquire new skills. They were waiting to learn of the living Christ, of God's love and of eternity. Why should not this project go forward? It was Spain's best assurance of safe and secure Pacific shores. But who was listening?

The days of festivity were soon over. One by one each ship set white sails against blue skies and drifted out of view. The quiet of abandoned hopes settled down on the striving community and the monotonous pattern of life resumed its rhythmical routine. Summer mellowed into fall.

Just before sailing time, Juan Pérez became seriously ill. Shipmates and landsmen pleaded with him to remain in Monterey but the seasoned mariner was determined to sail with his ship. Two days out of Monterey he died. A fellow Majorcan, one of Serra's best friends and one of California's most resolute and conscientious heroes was gone, buried at sea, where he had spent most of his life. Time after time, the missionary project had hinged on the daring, proficiency and sagacity of this noble master mariner. Along with Portolá, Crespí, Palóu, Gálvez and Serra, Captain Juan Pérez should be remembered by historians as indispensable to the Spanish era in California.

Serra had again pressed the issue of founding new missions. Four of Palóu's Baja California priests still awaited assignments. Rivera's argument that he had too few soldiers was justified on the grounds that Bucareli had not sent the one hundred men he had promised. To offset this, Serra proposed that six of his guard at San Carlos could be spared and that San Diego could spare six more. With these men, they could found one mission at San Buenaventura. Rivera refused at first, but finally yielded to the padre's tenacious persuasion by a compromise. He would agree to founding one mission at San Juan Capistrano, halfway between San Gabriel and San Diego.

Serra's persistence, aside from religious zeal, was pure logic. Time was running out: his years were numbered; the Spanish government was showing every sign of weakness and lack of funds; colonists had begun to arrive by boat, and others were coming overland. In other localities an entire mission system had broken down because of a few troublesome colonists. Right now the Indians were well disposed toward the missions. If he could complete the California mission ladder without all these long interruptions, the Indians, trained in a variety of skills, could soon cope with the inevitable influx of colonists.

In accordance with Rivera's concession to found San Juan Capistrano, Fr. Lasuén (who had served under Serra in Baja and was one of the six who had come with Palóu), along with Sergeant Ortega from San Diego and twelve soldiers, arrived at the location selected for the mission on October 29, 1775. Lasuén raised the cross, blessed it and said the Mass of dedication. The natives showed every sign of friendliness and even offered to help with the work. In a short time, the corral for the livestock was completed and the foundations laid for the buildings. San Juan Capistrano seemed to be off to a fine start. Then word came of terror at San Diego.

Ortega and his men were to return at once. This meant that Capistrano must be abandoned, at least for the time. They buried the bells and other non-perishable supplies and rushed back to the scene of trouble.

A dissident, runaway mission Indian, named San Carlos, had led the uprising. He had poured out his grievances in explosive words, fused with hatred. The Spaniards would soon control all the tribes, he told the Indians of the outlying villages. They must kill, burn and run them out. His fiery words found sympathetic ears among those natives who were jealous of the better living conditions of the valley mission Indians. San Carlos, triumphant in his new feeling of leadership, proposed and organized a massive attack against the pitifully vulnerable mission.

There was a chill in the air, that night of November 5, 1775. The moon was bright. About eight hundred painted Indians, armed with bows and arrows, slithered down the slopes into the encampment on the flat land. They formed two groups. The first was to attack the guardhouse and presidio. The other would seize the mission about five miles away.

The first group surrounded the guardhouse, knocked out a guard and set a signal fire. Then their bravado evaporated. The rest of the guards were asleep, and so were all the soldiers inside the building, but for some reason the natives fled.

The other group descended on the mission at about 1:30 a.m. while everyone there was asleep. They looted the warehouse and sacristy, taking supplies, embroidered vestments, chalices and all the valuable goods that had been acquired with such pain. These they gave to the women to carry back to the villages, while the men set fire to the buildings. Constructed of logs, with thatched roofs, the buildings quickly exploded into flame. The two priests, a carpenter and the four soldiers on hand went into action. Using any solid barricade they could find, they fired into the mass of savages, spewing arrows all around. The carpenter was killed and two of the soldiers wounded, but the seven men drove off the swarms of Indians. Fr. Fuster, who fought beside the soldiers as burning beams were falling all around, wrote later, "That night seemed as long as the pains of purgatory."

Fr. Jayme, believing his presence would calm the savages, went into the open, calling out, "Amar a Dios, hijos," ("Love God, my children"). These were his last words. The Indians seized him, stripped off all clothing but his underwear, shot numerous arrows into his body, then brutally pounded his face with rocks and clubs. Fr. Luís Jayme, a Majorcan, was the first missionary martyr of California.

No doubt San Carlos had deliberately staged the rebellion during Ortega's absence. Without him, military discipline was relaxed—the presidio guards hold the historic distinction of sleeping through the entire melee. Communication between the mission and the presidio by means of bells and bugle calls was a daily routine. But on this particular night, nothing—neither fire nor gunshot nor savage shrieks—had disturbed the military.

News of the disaster did not reach Rivera at Monterey until December 15, a month and eight days afterward. At once the commander personally took the message to Serra at Carmel. Rivera was fiercely angry and demanded reprisals equal to the violence of the crime. Serra, on the other hand, realized that severe punishment would only lead to more violence. It was useless to reason with Rivera in his present trauma, but Serra prepared to go to San Diego. Fr. Fuster needed his advice and consolation, and Serra could prevent drastic reprisals. Knowing this, Rivera refused a military escort for the missionary president who had to remain in Monterey. With ten soldiers Rivera set out for San Diego himself, joining up at San Gabriel with Captain Juan Bautista de Anza, who had just arrived overland with a group of colonists. With seventeen of his men, Anza accompanied Rivera and his ten men to the troubled mission.

By February, Anza felt he had served the cause of San Diego and returned to his colonists at San Gabriel. Actually, the Spaniards had feared that Indians of the back country, perhaps thousands, might have been involved. However, it seems more probable that the uprising was limited to those Indians who had heard the fiery voice of San Carlos. At any rate, there was no further trouble.

Anza and his group proceeded northward, receiving an enthusiastic welcome at each mission with "the festive peal of the good bells."[1]

By early April, Rivera's reprisals were reaching a climax in San Diego. San Carlos, after months of long, cumbersome trials, admitted it was he who had led the revolt. But he sought sanctuary in the temporary church. The padres had no desire to defend the culprit, but church sanctuary, by tradition and by canon law, was a sacred thing. This they would defend with their lives.

Rivera was determined. In defiance of Church law and admonitions of the padres, he, with a military guard, forced his way into the church and seized the offender.

Nine months after the disaster, Serra took passage on the *San Antonio* and arrived in San Diego. At the sight of the Father-president, Rivera shuddered. He knew he had disobeyed every rule of the *Representación;* he had defied Bucareli's orders; he had thwarted the mission project which he had been assigned to assist and defend. Would Serra go to Mexico City, as he had in the case of Fages?

Yet, agitated though he was, Rivera added one more black mark to his record.

Captain Diego de Chaquet of the *San Antonio* could see that San Diego needed new buildings and offered the help of his twenty sailors for the time they were in port. As long as Rivera would furnish the armed guard, the sailors would work with the priests and Indians in the reconstruction of the mission. The offer was accepted, and the task force made seven thousand adobe bricks and laid foundations for the new buildings in

1. Fr. Font's Diary, Bolton, *Anza's California Expedition,* pp. 392-395.

only eighteen days. A few more days of this organized plan of work would have completed the job. But Rivera heard rumors of Indian uprisings, or used this as an excuse. He ordered the military guard back to the presidio and refused to supply another. No uprising materialized, and the *San Antonio* sailed away, leaving the work to the slow process of native labor.

Military reinforcements came from Loreto, and Rivera had no alternative but to rebuild San Diego, reestablish San Juan Capistrano and establish the San Francisco missions.

On November 1, 1776, Serra sang the high Mass of dedication, and California's seventh mission—at San Juan Capistrano—was reestablished. The sixth, Mission San Francisco—which later came to be known as Mission Dolores—had been founded in the interim, on October 9, three months after the colonies on the east coast had signed the Declaration of Independence.

Santa Clara, the eighth mission of the chain, was founded on January 12, 1777, and the pueblo of San José, nearby, was settled by Anza's colonists.

By 1777, eight years after her beginning, Alta California had surpassed Baja in growth and stature. Eight missions were growing and prospering, and California had become an institution. Nothing could stop her progress now.

Three years earlier, in 1774, Gálvez had suggested that Monterey should become the capital of both the Californias and that the governor should reside there. That same year, Bucareli appointed Felipe de Neve as Governor of California. Since Gálvez' suggestion had not yet become official, Neve resided in Loreto, but was instructed to maintain friendly relations with the commander and the priests of both provinces.

In August, 1775, orders from the king made Monterey the official capital of the province, and Neve was informed that he should reside there, but he did not receive the orders until December, 1776. He arrived in February, 1777. The new governor's first official act was to visit the president of the California missions, Fr. Junípero Serra, at Carmel.

"A new optimism runs through [Serra's] letters during the ensuing months which recalls the ebulient spirit of those first ones written from Monterey peninsula in 1770,"[2] writes Fr. Geiger. Rivera was appointed Lieutenant Governor, with residence at Loreto.

---

2. Geiger, *op. cit.,* Vol. II, p. 147.

The Bells
Toll

In the eighteenth century, Confirmation, one of the Seven Sacraments of the Catholic Church, was usually administered by a bishop. However, on occasion, where a bishop was not available, the privilege could be extended to missionary priests.

When Serra was assigned to Baja California in 1768, he learned that the privilege had been given to the president of the Jesuit missions there. Accordingly, he petitioned, through his Franciscan College of San Fernando, for the same privilege. Rome granted the permission in 1774, but all appointments of the Church were subject to approval by the Spanish government. Consequently, the papers gathered dust on official desks while Christian Indians were passing on to the next world without benefit of the sacrament.

Four years after Rome's approval, the *Santiago*, which anchored in San Francisco Bay, brought the official document empowering Serra to administer the sacrament for a period of ten years. Only six of the ten years were left. It had long been Serra's hope to bestow on every baptized California Christian the grace of the Holy Spirit through this sacrament. Now that he had the power, he was determined to lose no time.

In the simple language they understood, he had related to the natives the meaning and purpose of Baptism. Perhaps they failed to comprehend the theology, but due to the wonderful harmony between the sacraments and human nature, the basic truths found recognition: that they could become children of God; that in their world of needs and problems, Baptism gave them assurance of the protective guidance of a loving Father—God; that by virtue of their humanity, they were qualified to love their neighbor and love their God. The signs, the formalities, the symbols, as well as the words of the sacrament, witnessed to the ultimate truth of the Incarnation: that Christ was indeed alive and present among them, waiting to be recognized. Through the teaching, the prayers, the songs, they gradually grew in awareness of the love of God for them and felt, in return, their love and supplication going out to him in trust and faith.

Christianization lifts a human being to the knowledge of Christ. It opens to him or her the knowledge that each person is a free and responsible individual with special dignity and the right to perfect his or her talents and to live in the hope of an eternal home and destiny.

As baptized members of the mission community, with the Church as its center, the Indians had made progress. Now, Serra hoped that through the Sacrament of Confirmation they would receive further strength— the spiritual strength of the Holy Spirit, a grace needed individually and collectively for the maturing of their

Christian faith. He would leave with them the sacra-
mental grace for their coming-of-age.

We have followed the Majorcan from infancy
through an exemplary life of faith and courage: the
simplicity of his inspirationally religious home life; the
total giving of himself to the love of God in his calling
to the priesthood; the perseverance and consummate
dedication through his training years; the brilliant success of his teaching, which resulted in unsought renown; the zealous fulfillment of that love and selfless
dedication in his missionary career. We have felt with
him hope and disappointment; joy and sorrow; frustration and suffering. We have seen that he endured each
cross with Christlike patience, humility and peace.
Fr. Serra's acceptance of the gray robe of St. Francis
had been no immature formality, no following of a
pattern of style or custom, no pretense or sophistication. His was a true priestly vocation.

In his travels to administer the Sacrament of Confirmation, Fr. Serra revealed, as never before, his true
self: his consecration to prayer; his constant self-
sacrifice, never compromising with human comforts;
his simplicity; and above all, the sincerity of his love
for Christ and for those he had come to serve. He
deeply and totally loved souls, and he clearly felt an
obligation to administer the sacrament to each of the
Indians in his care. It was, in a way, his last will and
testament to them—his gift of grace from God, through
him to them, to strengthen and sustain them with divine guidance and mercy.

In this spirit he began his tour, first at San Carlos,
his home mission. The word filtered through the mission; the bells rang assembly and all the families came
to the church. The priests heard confessions; then,
assisted by Frs. Crespí and Dumetz, Serra sang the high

Mass with solemnity and dignity. The congregation joined in the singing and prayers, and the padre spoke to them, simply explaining profound truths, partly in Spanish and partly in their own tongue. Confirmations followed.

In August, he sailed on the *Santiago* to San Diego, where he spent twelve days confirming, repeating the ceremony of San Carlos. Then, by land, he "climbed the ladder" of missions—San Juan Capistrano, San Gabriel, San Luís Obispo, San Antonio—arriving home just two days before Christmas. Since June, he had confirmed 1,897 persons.

By 1779, San Francisco had become the favored harbor, leaving Monterey more or less deserted. In fact, as Serra planned his Confirmation tour to the San Francisco Bay area, two ships were lying at anchor there— two more exploration vessels. They had sailed together from San Blas and had reached Alaska. Both captains and chaplains were anxious to see the famous Fr. Serra and waited in port for his coming.

The old leg infection became so acute that Serra at first sent word he must postpone the trip. Then his determination overcame his agony and he journeyed to Santa Clara and on to Mission Dolores. At each mission, after singing high Mass and preaching a fervent sermon, he confirmed all baptized adults who had not received the sacrament. Thirty-nine seamen received Confirmation, besides forty-nine soldiers and 101 Indians and their families.

During the long ceremonies, Serra seemed oblivious to the pain, but when the doctors examined his inflamed leg, they said it was a miracle that he could even stand on it. He would not submit to treatment for which we do not blame him. Eighteenth-century medical science was far from a panacea for pain or infection.

While Serra was in San Francisco, word came that Spain, again at war with England, was, through her alliance with France, helping the American colonies fight for freedom.

Serra had his own problems of freedom. Governor Neve, a man who insisted on technicalities and "fine print interpretations" had questioned Serra's papers authorizing his right to confirm.

Ultimately, after almost two years had passed, Neve's scruples regarding Serra's right to confirm were resolved. On August 16, 1781, Serra received letters reestablishing his permission to administer the sacrament.

As he had done before, Serra started confirming at home base, then took to the road again. First he visited the northern missions—San Antonio, Santa Clara and San Francisco. For Fr. Crespí, who accompanied him, this was in a sense, a sentimental journey. It was his first sight of San Francisco since his discovery expedition with Portolá in 1769, and he was delighted to see his old schoolmate and lifelong friend Fr. Palóu again. For Fr. Crespí, the trip was one of those mysterious gifts that eludes definition; there was a bit of prediction about it, for a few days after their return to Carmel, Crespí became seriously ill and on January 1, 1782, he died. Crespí, who had been in Alta since the first expedition in 1769, will be known in history as the diarist of the Spanish conquest of the west. He had participated in and left detailed accounts of all the major explorations. Besides the Portolá expeditions, he had traveled with Fages through the San Joaquin Valley and had been the diarist on the first sea exploration of Alaska. All together, his travels had covered more miles than Coronado's, and his narration of the scenes, topography, people and experiences are invaluable to history.

From the time he entered the monastery of San Francisco in Palma, Serra had been his model. Many of the years he spent in the New World, teaching, baptizing, training, had been spent beside or near his former instructor and model. Serra buried the body of his beloved friend, pupil and fellow missionary in the sanctuary of the Church of San Carlos at Carmel, where it lies today.

When Neve had taken office, he had been ordered to establish communities of settlers. Ideally, colonists from Mexico, supported for a time by the government, would engage in farming and produce food for themselves and the military. Consequently, on September 4, 1781, Neve founded the village of Los Ángeles. Named for the Blessed Virgin, it was called Nuestra Señora de los Ángeles, Our Lady of the Angels. Not far from San Gabriel, it was the beginning of the great metropolis of the west.

Unfortunately, many of the first settlers did not succeed in carrying out their planned function. In fact, the missions supplied food for themselves, the military and the colonists. Not trained or qualified for the rigors of frontier life nor provided with competent leaders, most of the colonists eventually returned to Mexico. Some, however, survived and established roots for others to come. The site was well chosen, as is confirmed by the busy, roaring city of today.

Serra was touring the southern missions, confirming, advising and encouraging his fellow missionaries, when Neve received orders to found three missions in the long-neglected Santa Barbara area. The Chumas and Canalino Indians had been of special interest to Serra since the beginning. He had never ceased to plead for missions for these people. On Easter Sunday, March 31, 1782, it was Serra's great joy to bless the site, raise the cross and say the Mass of dedication for San Buenaventura, the ninth mission and Serra's last. No governor could refuse to found a mission ordered by the viceroy, but he could delay its founding. San Buenaventura, the third mission Gálvez had ordered to be founded in 1769, had truly been delayed by the succession of governors. Serra's hope of thirteen years had at last been realized.

Santa Barbara was established a month later, "this new mission and Royal Presidio of Santa Barbara." Actually, Santa Barbara was a presidio only. Neve was in fact opposed to the mission system and would not set a date for the founding of the Santa Barbara mission. This was, of course, a grave disappointment to Serra. Furthermore, a third mission ordered by the civil authorities in the Santa Barbara Channel area was but a dream.

Before his right to confirm would expire, Serra was determined to make one more round of the missions. He was suffering from acute bronchitis, and friends advised against such a long, arduous journey. But his anxiety to bring the grace of the sacrament to his "children" superseded regard for his health. In June, 1783, he boarded the ship *La Favorita* and sailed to San Diego. After having administered the sacrament there he went to San Gabriel, where he became seriously ill. Still he continued to say Mass, baptize and confirm.

Then he went on to the new mission of San Buenaventura, a source of great joy and satisfaction, then to the presidio at Santa Barbara, after which he continued on to San Luís Obispo, San Antonio and home. He remained at San Carlos four months before going on to Santa Clara and San Francisco. Returning by way of Santa Clara again, he dedicated a new church. All of this would have taxed the energy of a younger, hardier man. Since receiving permission to confirm in June, 1778, Serra had administered the sacrament to 5,275 persons.

At Santa Clara, Serra felt that death was near. He rested a few days, then asked Palóu to stay with him. He made his confession, spent the days in spiritual exercises and returned to San Carlos, where he arrived on May 26, 1784.

Fr. Serra had made his last journey. He could look upon the accomplishments of the last fifteen years with gratitude. Despite disappointments, harassments, delays and dissent, Alta California now had nine missions, four presidios and two pueblos. Cattle in abundance roamed the fertile lands. The missions not only supplied for their own needs but had a surplus. Prosperity had supplanted poverty and starvation.

In a land where the name of Jesus had never before been heard, there was now a climate of Christianity. Each day began and closed with the ringing of the bells, calling people to prayer. Mass was the first activity of the day—the Mass in which, according to Catholic faith, the living Christ, Redeemer of mankind, was present on the altar and afterwards remained present in the Blessed Sacrament.

The Christian message as related to the natives had given them the knowledge that each was a unique person loved by God. The Indians had learned that God heard their prayers for guidance and protection and that life was more than a search for fish and acorns. And they had learned from the example of the padres that peace was better than killing, stealing and the disruption of the social order.

"Amar a Dios," "Vaya con Dios," "Bienvenidos, Amigos," the watchwords of the new civilization, centered attention on the peoples' love of God, their dependence and trust in him, and their love for each other in a Christian sense. Although the missionary project had fallen far short of Serra's dreams, hopes and goals, still he held no bitterness, only gratitude.

Several weeks after his return to San Carlos, Serra sent for Fr. Palóu. When Palóu arrived on August 18, the padre was not only suffering severe discomfort from his bronchial pneumonia, but the infected leg was extremely inflamed and swollen. Still Serra prayed and followed his spiritual exercises as though he were in good health. Palóu chanced to remark to one of the soldiers, "It does not seem that the Father-president is very sick." The soldier replied, "Father, there is no basis for hope. He is ill. The saintly priest is always well when it comes to praying and singing, but he is nearly finished."[1]

For a few days the two Majorcan friends talked of many things. Serra kept the conversation on mission problems: the shortage of priests from Spain, the new diocese of Sonora, with jurisdiction over California, the delays of founding new missions. In a way, he was briefing his interim successor. Though these problems were vexing, Serra had faced greater ones. His trust in the providence of Almighty God and his calm, inner peace transmitted to Palóu the fortitude he needed now and would need in the days to come.

The *San Carlos* dropped anchor at Monterey. The ship's doctor immediately came to examine the missionary president. As was the medical practice of the day, he cauterized Serra's chest, adding to the pain and still not diminishing the illness.

One afternoon an old Indian woman asked to see the padre. Serra patiently listened to her woes, which seemed chiefly to be that she was cold, then gave her a

---

1. James, *op. cit.,* p. 266.

blanket. Later it was learned that he had torn his only blanket in two and had given half to the eighty-year-old Indian woman.

For over a week the Father–president suffered extreme difficulty in breathing. Still he made no complaints. On the morning of August 27, he arose at dawn as usual and recited his breviary. He asked Palóu to give him Viaticum, the last sacrament of the Church. But rather than having Palóu bring it to him, he insisted on going to the church. Wearing a white stole over his gray habit, he walked to the church, entered the sanctuary and knelt on a prie-dieu prepared for him. He sang the *Tantum Ergo* with full, firm voice, and received general absolution and the sacred Host. After some time in prayer, he returned to his room.

Sleep was impossible that night because of the intense pain. He knelt beside his narrow plank bed, with his chest pressed against the rough boards, and spent the long hours in prayer and meditation.

The next morning he had company. The officers of the *San Carlos,* his good friends of many years, had come to pay their respects. First, he asked that the bells ring in their honor, then he arose and greeted the men in his usual cordial, gracious manner, giving no sign that he was seriously ill.

About noon he asked Palóu to read the deathbed prayers. For a time he had been shaken by a great fear, then he told Palóu, "Thanks be to God! Thanks be to God! All fear has left me. I have no fear. Let us go outside."[2] At siesta, he lay down on the rough boards that were his bed, covered himself with the half blanket and placed the crucifix on his breast. After lunch Palóu looked in to see if his friend needed anything. "I

---

2. *Ibid.,* p. 271.

found him as we had left him a little before, but now asleep in the Lord."[3]

That afternoon the bells of San Carlos Mission tolled the solemn, mournful, monotones of death. Quickly, the news spread. Fr. Junípero Serra, president of the California missions, was dead. Spaniards, Indians, half-breeds, soldiers, sailors—all came to pay respects to "Santo Padre, Bendito Padre," the "Saintly Father, the Good, Blessed Father."

Six hundred Indians attended the funeral the next morning. They came from Carmel, Monterey, San Antonio and the outlying villages to pray for the padre they loved. All those who had come the day before and many others paid tribute to the great missionary whose reputation now extended throughout most of New Spain. The ship's cannons fired "Salute," echoed by the bells' solemn tolling of "Doble," the mournful song of death. Fr. Palóu sang the solemn Funeral Mass and delivered an affectionate, moving sermon. Then they buried the Majorcan, who had left his home half-a-world away to bring Christ's message of love and mercy to the native American. His body was placed in the San Carlos sanctuary next to Fr. Crespí's.

For him was not the glorification of renown but the loneliness and hunger of a remote frontier; not the ease and comfort of an establishment but half a blanket on a straw mattress and plank bed; not an ermine-trimmed robe but sandals and a cross.

Serra had lived in California only fifteen years, but his work was the beginning of something greater than mission walls. The twenty-one missions that grew and prospered along El Camino Real eventually crumbled. But their message never died.

---

3. *Ibid.*, p. 272.

If at first in San Diego, the bells rang out in an empty world, their song reached hearts and souls later to come. Primitive men came, heard and believed. Freed from the slavery of ignorance, hunger and savagery, they learned a better way of life. In the mission, the Indian found protection, food, clothing, understanding and the freedom of a son of God.

On August 28, 1784, the Apostle of California and one of America's great men slipped from this world into the infinite freedom of his God, but his brilliant example of hope, courage and faith established on the western shores of our continent a civilization that would blend into the American scene. As the colonists of the east were fighting for the Christian principles of independence, Serra was securing in California the ideal of man's dignity as a child of God and his right as an individual to pursue his talents. His memory lives on, as do his fortitude and his sanctity.

Alta California Missions
Founded by Fr. Junípero Serra

July 16, 1769	San Diego
June 3, 1770	San Carlos de Borromeo at Monterey
July 14, 1771	San Antonio de Padua
August 24, 1771	San Carlos de Borromeo moved to Carmel
September 8, 1771	San Gabriel
September 1, 1772	San Luís Obispo
October 29, 1775	San Juan Capistrano
November 1, 1776	San Juan Capistrano, reestablished
October 9, 1776	San Francisco de Asís, Mission Dolores
January 12, 1777	Santa Clara
March 31, 1782	San Buenaventura

Bibliography

Baer, Kurt, and Rudinger, Hugo P. *Architecture of the California Missions*. Berkeley, CA: University of California Press, 1958.

Berger, John A. *The Franciscan Missions of California*. Garden City, NY: Doubleday and Co., Inc., 1948.

Bauer, Helen. *California Mission Days*. Garden City, NY: Doubleday and Co., Inc., 1951.

————. *California Rancho Days*. Garden City, NY: Doubleday and Co., Inc., 1953.

Bolton, Herbert Eugene. *Anza's California Expedition*, 5 vols. Berkeley, CA: University of California Press, 1930.

————. *Fray Juan Crespí, Missionary Explorer on the Pacific Coast*. Berkeley, CA: University of California Press, 1927.

————. *Coronado—Knight of Pueblos and Plains*. New York, NY: Whittlesey House, 1949.

————. *Fray Francisco Palóu*, Vols. I, II, III, IV.

————. *Historical Memoirs of New California*, ed. H. E. Bolton. Translated. From Manuscripts in Archives, Mexico. Berkeley, CA: University of California Press, 1926.

————. *Missions as a Frontier in the Spanish American Colonies*. El Paso, TX: Western College Press, 1960.

————. *Rim of Christendom*. New York, NY: The Macmillan Co., 1936.

————. *Padre on Horseback*. San Francisco, CA: The Sonora Press, 1932.

————. *Spanish Explorations of the Southwest*. New York, NY: C. Scribner's Sons, 1916.

Brandt, J. A. *Toward the New Spain*. Chicago, IL: University of Chicago Press, 1933.

Bro, Bernard, O.P. *The Spirituality of the Sacraments*. New York, NY: Sheed and Ward, 1968.

Buell, R. *California Stepping Stones*. Palo Alto, CA: Stanford University Press, 1948.

Cannon, Ray and Sunset Editors. *Sea of Cortez*. Menlo Park, CA: Lane Magazine and Book Co., 1966.

Chapman, Charles Edward. *Founding of Spanish California*. New York, NY: Macmillan Co., 1921.

————. *History of Spain*. New York, NY: Macmillan Co., 1918.

————. *Colonial Hispanic America*. New York, NY: Macmillan Co., 1933.

Chevignard, B. M., O.P. *Reconciled with God*. New York, NY: Sheed and Ward, 1967.

Cicognani, Amleto Giovanni. *Sanctity in America*. Paterson, NJ: St. Anthony Guild, 1939.

Corle, Edwin. *The Gila, River of the Southwest*. New York, NY: Rinehart (Holt, Rinehart and Winston, University of Nebraska Press, Lincoln, NE), 1951.

Collins, W. *Cathedral Cities of Spain*. New York, NY: Dodd and Mead, Co., 1909.

Cullen, Rev. Th. F. *Spirit of Serra*. New York, NY: Spiritual Books Associated, 1935.

Daniel-Rops, Henri. *Cathedral and Crusade*. New York, NY: E. P. Dutton and Co., Inc., 1957.

Dawson, H. Christopher. *The Formation of Christendom*. New York, NY: Sheed and Ward, 1964.

Diez, Del Corral. *Majorca*. New York, NY: Norton, 1963.

Duffus, R. L. *The Santa Fe Trail*. New York, NY: Tudor Publishing Co., 1963.

Englehardt, Zephrin, O.F.M. *The Franciscans in California*. Harbor Springs, MI: Holy Childhood Indian School, 1897.

————. *The Missions and Missionaries of California*. San Francisco, CA: James H. Barry Co., 1916.

————. *Santa Barbara Mission*. San Francisco, CA: James H. Barry Co., 1923.

————. *San Carlos de Borromeo*. Santa Barbara, CA: The Schauer Printing Studio, Inc., 1934.

Farrell, Walter, O.P. *A Companion to the Summa,* 4 vols. New York, NY: Sheed and Ward, 1945-1951.

Fitch, A. H. *Junípero Serra*. Chicago, IL: McClurg and Co., 1914.

Garces, Francisco. *On the Trail of a Spanish Pioneer, Diary of an Itinerary Priest*. New York, NY: F. P. Harper, 1930. Revised, San Francisco, CA: J. Howell Books, 1965.

Gardner, Earle Stanley. *The Hidden Heart of Baja*. New York, NY: Wm. Morrow Co., 1968.

————. *Hovering over Baja*. New York, NY: Wm. Morrow Co., 1962.

Geiger, Maynard J., O.F.M., Ph.D. *The Life and Times of Junípero Serra*. Academy of American Franciscan History, Richmond, VA: The Wm. Byrd Press, Inc., 1959.

————. *Palóu's Life of Fray Junípero Serra*, Trans. with Notes. Academy of American Franciscan History, Richmond, VA: The William Byrd Press Inc., 1955.

Gemelli, Agostino. *The Franciscan Message to the World*. London: Burns, 1934.

Hielscher, Kurt. *Picturesque Spain*. New York, NY: Brentano's, 1924.

Horgan, Paul. *Conquistadors*. New York, NY: Farrar, Strauss and Co., 1963.

───── . *The Great River—The Rio Grande*. New York, NY: Holt, Rinehart and Winston, 1954.

───── . *The Indians and Spain*.

───── . *Mexico and the United States*. Pleasantville, NY: Funk and Wagnels, Div. Readers' Digest Books, Inc., 1954-1968.

Hoffman, L. B. *California Beginnings*. San Francisco, CA: Harr Wagner, 1933.

Hurlimann, Martin. *Spain*. New York, NY: Viking Press, 1964.

James, George Wharton. *Palóu's Life of Junípero Serra*, Trans. Pasadena, CA: George Wharton James, 1913.

Kroeber, Alfred Louis. *Handbook of the Indians of California*. Berkeley, CA: California Book Co., Ltd., 1953.

Krutch, Joseph Wood. *Baja California and the Geography of Hope*. San Francisco, CA: Sierra Club Press, 1967.

Lummis, Charles Fletcher. *Spanish Pioneer and California Missions*. Chicago, IL: A. C. McClurg and Co., 1929.

Madariaga, Salvador de. *Spain, a Modern History*. New York, NY: Frederick A. Praeger, Publishers, 1958.

Mais, S. P. B. and Gillian Mais. *Majorcan Holiday*. Freeport, NY: Books for Libraries Press, 1968.

Maass. *The Dream of Phillip II*. Indianapolis, NY: Bobbs-Merrill Co., 1945.

Maynard, Theodore. *The Long Road*. New York, NY: Appleton-Century-Crofts, Inc., 1954.

O'Brien, Eric. *Apostle of California—Padre Serra*. Los Angeles, CA: The Tidings Press, 1944.

Prescott, W. H. *History of the Reign of Phillip II*. Philadelphia, PA: J. B. Lippencott Co., 1887.

———. *History of the Conquest of Mexico*. Philadelphia, PA: D. McKay, 1893.

Repplier, Agnes. *Junípero Serra, Pioneer Colonist of California*. Garden City, NY: Doubleday and Doran Co., Inc., 1933.

Reynolds, James. *Fabulous Spain*. New York, NY: G. P. Putnam's Sons, 1953.

Richman, Irving B. *California Under Spain and Mexico*. Boston and New York, NY: Houghton-Mifflin Co., 1911.

Salter, Cedric. *Introducing Spain*. New York, NY: Sloane Co., 1953.

Shippen, Katherine B. *New Found World*. New York, NY: The Viking Press, 1945. Revised 1964.

Smith, Rhea Marsh. *Spain*. Ann Arbor, MI: University of Michigan Press, 1965.

Solhenitzn, Aleksander I. *The First Circle*, Trans. from Russian, T. P. Whitney. New York, NY: Harper and Row, 1968.

Tibesar, Antonine, O.F.M., Ph.D. *Writings of Junípero Serra*, 3 vols. Academy of American Franciscan History, Washington, D.C., Baltimore, MD: J. H. Furst Co., 1956.

Walsh, Marie T. *The Mission Bells of California*. San Francisco, CA: Harr Wagner Publishing Co., 1934.

Waxman, Percy. *What Price Majorca*. New York, NY: Farrar and Rinehart Inc., 1933.

———. *The California Missions*. ed. Paul C. Johnson. Menlo Park, CA: Lane Magazine and Book Co., 1968.

ST. PAUL BOOK & MEDIA CENTERS
OPERATED BY THE DAUGHTERS OF ST. PAUL

ALASKA
750 West 5th Ave., Anchorage, AK 99501 **907-272-8183.**

CALIFORNIA
3908 S. Sepulveda Blvd., Culver City, CA 90230 **213-202-8144.**
1570 Fifth Ave. (at Cedar Street), San Diego, CA 92101 **619-232-1442.**
46 Geary Street, San Francisco, CA 94108 **415-781-5180.**

FLORIDA
Coral Park Shopping Center, 9808 S.W. 8 St., Miami, FL 33174
305-559-6715; 305-559-6716.

HAWAII
1143 Bishop Street, Honolulu, HI 96813 **808-521-2731.**

ILLINOIS
172 North Michigan Ave., Chicago, IL 60601 **312-346-4228; 312-346-3240.**

LOUISIANA
423 Main Street, Baton Rouge, LA 70802 **504-343-4057; 504-336-1504.**
4403 Veterans Memorial Blvd., Metairie, LA 70006 **504-887-7631;
504-887-0113.**

MASSACHUSETTS
50 St. Paul's Ave., Jamaica Plain, Boston, MA 02130 **617-522-8911.**
Rte. 1, 450 Providence Hwy., Dedham, MA 02026 **617-326-5385.**

MISSOURI
1001 Pine Street (at North 10th), St. Louis, MO 63101 **314-621-0346.**

NEW JERSEY
Hudson Mall, Route 440 and Communipaw Ave.,
Jersey City, NJ 07304 **201-433-7740.**

NEW YORK
625 East 187th Street, Bronx, NY 10458 **212-584-0440.**
59 East 43rd Street, New York, NY 10017 **212-986-7580.**
78 Fort Place, Staten Island, NY 10301 **718-447-5071; 718-447-5086.**

OHIO
616 Walnut Street, Cincinnati, OH 45202 **513-421-5733.**
2105 Ontario Street (at Prospect Ave.), Cleveland, OH 44115
216-621-9427.

PENNSYLVANIA
1719 Chestnut Street, Philadelphia, PA 19103 **215-568-2638;
215-864-0991.**

SOUTH CAROLINA
243 King Street, Charleston, SC 29401 **803-577-0175.**

TEXAS
114 Main Plaza, San Antonio, TX 78205 **512-224-8101.**

VIRGINIA
1025 King Street, Alexandria, VA 22314 **703-549-3806.**

WASHINGTON
2301 Second Ave. (at Bell), Seattle, WA 98121 **206-441-4100.**

CANADA
3022 Dufferin Street, Toronto 395, Ontario, Canada.